CW01626485

TALES OF A CHURCH MOUSE

In *Tales of a Church Mouse* the Revd Alec Shearwood uses an endearing group of Church Mice — with the odd intervention of Field Mice and other 'families' — to promote all the good tidings of his religion.

In fifty stories, many quite funny, some slightly tragic, but all with a message for 'the young at heart of all ages', the author has produced a book to delight everyone.

TALES OF A CHURCH MOUSE

FOR THE YOUNG AT HEART OF ALL AGES

Revd Alec Shearwood

Illustrations by Edward Taylor.

MERLIN BOOKS LTD.
Braunton Devon

©Alec Shearwood, 1987
First published in Great Britain, 1987

ISBN 0 86303 363-6
Printed in England by Antony Rowe Ltd., Chippenham, Wilts.

CONTENTS

The tales in this book all appeared, in a slightly different form, in the Magazine of the Wickenby Group of Parishes — eight small country parishes in Lincolnshire.

My thanks are due to the patient and long-suffering parishioners for their help over many years, without which these tales would never have been written.

I would like to add that any resemblance to an actual event or person is unintentional, but that would not be quite true!

Alec Shearwood

May I introduce myself and my family? My name is William and I am a mouse, and because we have always lived in Churches we are called Church Mice. Sometimes I find it rather lonely for I am fond of company, and enjoy telling people what is going on in my home and in the villages round about. Once an uncle of mine said, "He's too fond of the sound of his own voice!" but I didn't take any notice of *him*! And when I was very small my mother used to say, "Little mice should be seen and not heard," but that always seemed to be a very silly idea!

Anyway to cut a long tale short — oh dear, that does sound very painful — I never do seem to have enough people to talk to, and so sometimes I just talk to myself. One day last week I said to myself, "Why not write to people who would like to hear about us Church Mice?" And at once I answered myself "Why not?" So here goes.

I am only a very little mouse and I cannot write very well, but I will do my best. When I went to school I remember the Mistress Mouse telling me, "Every story must have a beginning, a middle and an end, just as every mouse must have a nose, a tummy and a tail." This seems to be all tummy, but perhaps that is a good thing, because our tummies are so important, aren't they? I seem to spend most of my time trying to find food to fill mine up.

I live in a village called Wickenby, and I have lots of brothers and sisters, and uncles and aunts who live in all the Churches around here. There is Horace of Holton who is a funny old uncle; he lives in a flat up the tower of Holton Church; he loves good food and brightly coloured clothes, and he waxes his whiskers! Then there's my brother Freddie of Friesthorpe; he used to have rather an eye for the girls until he married young Phoebe from Faldingworth. Aunt Sarah lives in Snelland Church with her two children who are named after famous film stars, Mickie and Minnie. Sister Lucy of Lissington is rather prim and proper. And Sir Bertram de Buslingthorpe, known to his friends as Bertie comes from a very old and grand family, and he lives in Buslingthorpe Church. Last, but not least, in the ancient Church of Snarford, behind a monument of a knight in armour, lives my Grandfather Sebastian; he is very old, rather fierce, and does not like company.

You see we are a big family. As we live in Churches we often hear about God and how He loves us. But I'm afraid that we are not always as good as we should be, except Sister Lucy of course, and sometimes we do get into the most awful scrapes; so I look forward to telling you more about us and all the adventures which we have.

UNCLE HORACE AND JEZEBEL

Uncle Horace's Church is in the village of Holton-cum-Beckering. Like all our Churches it is old and full of nooks and crannies which seem to have been especially made for mice to hide in when they are in danger.

Uncle Horace is one of those mice who enjoys the best things to eat, and who is terribly fussy about how he looks. He always has a little piece of smelly soap with which he washes several times a day. Then he wears the most un-mouse-like clothes you every did see; narrow trousers and pointed shoes; waistcoats by the score, each a more vivid colour than the last; and brass buttons to do them up. But because he eats so much he is getting rather fat these days, and his brass buttons keep on popping off!

Well, one day Uncle Horace was sunning himself near to the open Church door; he had just enjoyed a huge dinner of Cheddar cheese, sweet biscuits and chocolates. As he sat there, patting his tummy and admiring his lavender coloured waistcoat, he thought he saw a movement in the grass beside the path. For a moment he watched to see what was there, and then suddenly with a loud squeak and a big jump he was off into the Church, crying out as he went, "Oh my! Oh my! Help!

It's Jezebel!" And so it was, Jezebel the cat!

Now it is easy to talk, but I am sure that if Uncle Horace had stayed still Jezebel would not have seen him. However, he was so frightened that he jumped up and ran along the aisle towards his home in the tower as fast as his legs would carry him, with Jezebel, who had seen him as soon as he moved, chasing him as fast as she could.

I don't know if you have ever tried to run as soon as you have finished a large meal, like a Christmas dinner, but Uncle Horace found that his legs simply would not move as fast as he told them. "Faster! Faster!" he yelled down to them, but they just didn't seem to hear, and the more he cried "Faster!" the slower they went. Even then his long pointed shoes kept on getting caught up in each other.

It seemed to Uncle Horace as he ran, that the devil himself was in that cat. "Perhaps she *is* the devil," he gasped to himself. "Oh how I wish I had not eaten so much! All that Cheddar cheese, and all those sweet biscuits, and all that chocolate make my feet feel like lead." If he had had time to think more as he ran, which he hadn't because Jezebel was getting closer all the time, he might have thought like this; 'If I spend too much time in just enjoying myself, and being greedy, then when temptation or danger comes along I will not have the strength to face them — nor the skill to escape them.' In fact he might well have remembered the words of Jesus, "Watch and pray, lest ye fall into temptation."

But all this time poor Uncle Horace was too frightened to say anything except "Faster! Faster!" as Jezebel was drawing nearer and nearer. When they reached the tower she was only a tail's length away, and he felt her hot breath upon his back. Then . . . as her claws reached out to catch him, Uncle Horace dived down his hole to safety.

"Oh my!" he gasped. "Oh my Cheddar cheese, but that was a narrow squeak!" And how right he was!

FREDDIE AND THE MOLE

A great story-teller called Aesop told how once upon a time a mouse, who in the past had been spared by a lion, found that same lion caught in a strong net, and how he gnawed through the ropes of the net and freed the lion.

Well, there are no lions in our Churchyards, but last week a young mole did get caught in some string under the hedge round Freddie's Churchyard in Friesthorpe.

The more the little mole struggled, the more did his long claws get entangled. His eyesight was not very good and he could not see which way to get rid of the string, while his strong sense of hearing and smelling were no help at all. The poor mole was really very frightened indeed, partly because he couldn't free himself, and partly because his nose and his ears both told him that prowling near by was one of those great white cats from the farm across the road.

Now it so happened that Freddie was just then going for a morning stroll, and as he went he heard a faint cry of, "Help! Help!" from beneath the hedge. In a moment he had found the little mole, and

quickly set about gnawing through the string that was holding him so firmly. But then Freddie also heard the soft tread of the great white cat, only a few yards away, and for a moment he hesitated.

"Shall I run away?" he asked himself, "after all, this mole is no friend of mine, I hardly know him," and he made as though to scurry off to the safety of his Church. But then he saw the frightened little face looking up at him, and he began to gnaw all the harder at the string, scratching himself on some sharp thorns as he did so.

The great white cat had heard the rustling of the two tiny creatures in the hedge, and was pacing up and down only a few feet away trying to find them. Gradually the tangles of string disappeared as Freddie worked at them, but gradually the cat came nearer and nearer! At last there was only one strand of string left holding the mole, but the cat was now only just on the other side of the hedge.

Once again Freddie longed to run for his life, and once again he worked on until at last, just as the cat spied them, the string gave way and the mole was free! As fast as their legs could carry them they ran through the grass towards the Church, while the great white cat forced his way through the thick hedge and leapt after them. It was a very near thing, but Freddie and the mole reached safety just in time, and the angry cat made his way slowly back to the farm, his great white tail swishing from side to side as he went.

We are told that Jesus has redeemed us. That is a long word, but I believe it means that Jesus bought us from the power of evil and set us free. My brother, Freddie of Friesthorpe risked his life to save the little mole from the great white cat, and he set him free; so in a way, he redeemed him from that cat. Jesus gave His life to save you and me, not from a great white cat, but from evil and badness. And He set us free, free to serve Him or not as we please.

MISTER YELLOWHAMMER

"A little bit of bread and no cheese." That is what I heard as I peeped out of my Church door one day last week. Who could it be, I wondered, that would say such a very odd thing? It didn't sound like any of my family, and it certainly wasn't the Rector! Then I saw, hopping about on the gravel path outside the porch, a pretty little brown bird with a speckled yellow head.

"Good-morning," I said, for although he was obviously a very strange creature I do like to be polite. "Good-morning," I repeated.

"A little bit of bread and no cheese . . . a little bit of bread and no cheese," he chirruped back.

"Well," I retorted, "can you not say anything else? What's your name?"

"I'm Mister Yellowhammer," he replied, "and of course I can say lots of other things; however the bird books tell people that all I can say is 'A little bit of bread and no cheese,' " and so I have to humour them, and pretend that they are right for fear of hurting their feelings."

"Well now, how strange," I said, "I would much prefer to say, 'A little bit of bread and lots of cheese!' " But before I had finished speaking the little yellowhammer fluttered away over the hedge on to the road, and I went back indoors to think of breakfast. I was very glad that I not only had a little bit of bread hidden away, but a tiny piece of cheese to go with it.

When I had finished the last crumbs, and was getting ready to go out to look for my dinner, I remembered the words that Jesus taught us to say, "Give us this day our daily bread." 'That's not so very different from what the yellowhammer said,' I thought. Bread without cheese; how very strange!

That afternoon I went to tea with my sister Lucy in Lissington Church, and I told her all about my visitor.

"Why do you think he says that?" I asked her, but she only laughed.

"I can't think that he really means it."

"Well then," I went on, "do you think that Jesus really meant it when He said, 'Give us this day our daily bread,' with no mention of cheese, or chocolate for that matter?"

"William," retorted Lucy rather severely, "when Jesus said 'bread', He meant all the food that we need to keep us healthy . . . . Bread was just His way of putting it."

"Perhaps you're right," I muttered.

Of course I know she was right really, and I know that God understands what we mean when we say "Give us this day our daily bread." None the less, if I dared, I would love to add, "And just a little bit of cheese — please!"

WHO PLAYS THE PIANO?

"When the cat's away, the mice will play." I expect that you have heard that saying, and I daresay that you know what it means! Last month the Rector and his family were away for a bit, and so I said to myself, "Now is the time to go across to the Rectory to visit my cousins who live there."

Well, I don't know whether I ought to call the Rector a cat, but certainly the mice were playing when he was away! They invited me to stay for tea, which was as good a meal as I have had for a long time. Afterwards I joined in a game of hide-and-seek, and during it I found myself inside the piano.

An old couple lived there, and they were glad to show me round; they were very proud of their home, and showed how, by jumping round in a certain way, different sounds could be heard as the hammers hit the different wires.

"But that is nothing," they said. "Sometimes when we are sitting down quietly of an evening, lots of these little hammers start hitting the wires all by themselves, and they make lovely music, such clever little hammers they are! There now!" they exclaimed, "have you ever heard of anything like that before?"

I was so surprised to find two old mice who could be quite so ignorant, and I tried to explain to them that the music did not come of its own accord, but only because someone outside the piano was playing it. However I don't think that they really believed me, and they probably still fancy that their home is a place of wonderful magic!

That night as I walked round my quiet old Church I thought, 'There are probably some people who are almost as ignorant as those two Piano Mice; people who think that the sky and stars, and the sun and moon, and this world of ours came into being of their own accord, just as those Piano Mice thought that the music just happened.'

I hope that you children are not quite so silly as that! You know that someone has to play the piano if it is to make music — it won't play itself, will it? And I hope that you know too, that there is Someone whom we call God, who made the world, and who gives life to boys and girls, as well as to little Church Mice, in fact to all His creatures.

Creatures is rather a funny word isn't it? You are creatures just as much as I am, and I don't mind being called one, so why should you? You are created by God, and so am I, and that means that we are His creatures, made by Him, and loved by Him.

SUMMER VISITORS

On Easter Eve, after the people had brought in the lovely spring flowers to decorate my Church, I went outside for a breath of fresh air; and then I heard it . . . . a busy twittering song high above my head, and there, circling and wheeling, round and round, up and down and round again they went. Flashing down out of the clear blue sky, and gliding swiftly over the Churchyard grass were my dear old friends the swallows.

Oh my fur and whiskers, but wasn't I glad to see them! Gone was winter with its snow and its cold that used to freeze my poor toes, and those eager darting swallows made me think of the summer that was almost upon us; summer with its long days of sunshine and its warm welcoming nights; summer with its promise of harvest days, and the chance to replenish our larders once again.

"Hallo, Church Mouse!" they twittered, as they rested for a moment on the telephone wires in the Rectory garden, "how goes it with you? Where have you been all this time?"

"Why, here of course," I replied. "But where have you been?"

"We've been to sunny Africa and back again," they sang. "We go there every year in the winter; as soon as we feel the summer slipping away, and the nights getting longer and colder, and the leaves turning brown on the trees; then we begin to long for the comforting warmth of Africa, and we're off for a winter's holiday!"

While the swallows fluttered up and down, and settled once more on the wires, never ceasing to chatter as they did so, I thought to myself of the long, dark and cheerless winter that had passed.

"Why did you come back?" I called up to them. "Why didn't you stay where the sun always shines?"

"Because when the winter has passed," they called back, "and the days in Africa become so hot and dusty, we think again of tall, leafy trees, of green fields and gardens. We think of our homes which we built against the walls of village buildings and in your Church porch. So we set off again on the long, long journey across the Mediterranean Sea, across France and the English Channel, over England itself, until we come home to Wickenby."

I wonder if you feel as I do, and wish that you had wings and could fly away across the world like the swallows? What fun it must be, but what an exciting adventure too, and how brave they are! I asked them how they managed to find their way back over hundreds of miles of land and sea to the very place they had left many months before.

"We don't understand ourselves," they twittered, "we just know that we will find our way, and that we will arrive safely at our journey's end."

I think that God has given these little birds something just as wonderful as their skill and strength . . . . He has given them a faith and trust in His care that we Church Mice might do well to copy.

CAUGHT IN A BRAMBLE

Aunt Sarah of Snelland's two young mice ran home from school the other day full of mischief as usual. It was very cold, and there were still pockets of snow in which they jumped and rolled. Mickie and Minnie are none too well behaved at the best of times, and the clear frosty weather had made them more high spirited than ever.

Then quite suddenly, Minnie stood still with her head on one side, listening intently.

"Ssh!" she whispered, "do you hear anything?" Mickie was listening too, and to both of them there came a sound, a sort of crying, so soft they scarcely heard it. Stealthily, remembering for once what Aunt Sarah had told them about the dangers of the unknown, they crept towards the sound. It seemed to come from where a trailing length of old bramble showed above a mound of snow.

"Look!" exclaimed Mickie, pointing; and there, in the bramble, they saw a tiny Field-mouse.

All thoughts of play and mischief had gone as the two young mice struggled to loose their little cousin from the cruel thorn that held him tight. At last he was free, but so cold, and so badly hurt by the bramble, that he could hardly walk. It was a long time later that a very weary Mickie and Minnie staggered into their home in Snelland Church supporting the poor Field-mouse between them.

Aunt Sarah quickly helped to bring him down into their hole, and put him to bed with heaps of feathers and dried grass to bring some warmth to his frozen body. For several days he lay very ill and they knew that the bitterly cold time he had spent caught in that bramble was still causing him a lot of pain.

One night, as Aunt Sarah was taking her turn to care for their patient, Mickie and Minnie went up into the Church; it was dark except that the moon was shining through one of the windows on to the wall above the pulpit, and in the small patch of light they saw the Crucifix hanging there.

It seemed to the two little mice that the Figure on the Cross was looking down and wanting to speak to them, so very quietly they crept towards it and listened. The words came so softly that they had to strain their ears to hear: "You have shown how suffering can sometimes bring me great happiness. Of course I was sad to see your little friend in pain, but that pain called forth your love and kindness, and that gave me great joy."

Just then the moon went behind a cloud, the Cross became hidden once more, and two very happy little mice went back to help their friend get well again.

GOD'S KINGDOM

It was late at night, but not at all dark, for up above me the moon hung in the sky like a great white cheese glowing with light, while all over the sky were countless twinkling stars.

'I wonder,' I thought to myself, 'I wonder if there are any little Church Mice up there?' And as I looked up into the sky, it seemed to me that I understood something of the wonder of God who made it all, something of His kingdom, His power and His glory. So it was that I made my way up the Church path, feeling very small in the middle of this greatness, but with my head full of the most wonderful thoughts, and bursting to tell someone of what I had discovered about the glory of God. Some people may say that you can see God's glory in a great Cathedral, or a mountain peak, or a golden sunset, but what are these things compared with the vision of unending space and countless worlds, each one fashioned by God Himself, that we can see in such a night sky as this? 'Here,' I thought, 'is the kingdom, and the power and the glory of God.'

As I stepped back inside the Church I heard a thin little voice coming from out of the shadows, "Ah, William, I'm going to spend the night here, for I really am too tired to walk home!"

"Grandfather," I said, "please do stay, but first come outside to see what I have to show you." The old mouse grumbled something about it being very late, and groused about being very tired, and complained about being dragged out into the cold night air, but he shuffled through the doorway none the less.

"There," I exclaimed pointing upwards, "doesn't that show more of the kingdom of God than anything you have ever seen?" As I said this I felt proud and clever and very full of learning, and so it was to my surprise that Grandfather didn't seem to be much impressed.

"Oh William," he mumbled, through his straggly grey whiskers, "you have a lot to learn! Come with me tomorrow, and I'll show you the kingdom of God."

Well, tomorrow soon came, and I walked the long miles to Snarford with Grandfather Sebastian. It was evening time before we reached his Churchyard, and went through the gate. To my surprise he turned off the path and led me through the grass until quite suddenly we saw a little bird, a lark it was, sitting on her nest in the grass before us.

"Now William my young fellow," said Grandfather, "don't you understand that the kingdom of God is to be found in the hearts of all His creatures, and where love is, there is His kingdom?"

I listened carefully to what the dear old mouse was saying, because for all his crotchety ways he is wise, and kind at heart.

"That little skylark," he went on, "is full of love for the babies which she is tending, and the kingdom of God, and His glory and power are more surely there than in the grandest sunset or a million stars. It is in our hearts, yours and mine little William, that God loves to reign as king."

IN TROUBLE WITH THE LAW

You may not believe it when I tell you that we mice have our Courts of Law, just as men and women do, in which we try mice who have been accused of doing something wrong.

Some time ago, Uncle Horace of Holton got himself 'into trouble' as we say, and we all went along to the Court in which he was going to be tried to see how he would get on. The trial took place in a large room in the Hall, and we were told to sit down together at the back, and to keep quiet.

Presently Uncle Horace was brought in by two Police Mice, and oh, how he had changed! No longer did he strut around with that cocky and conceited air of his; no longer was he wearing his flashy clothes, but was in a very respectable suit — no doubt to impress the Judge!

Next, a fierce little mouse called upon us all to stand up as the Judge walked in. I had never seen a Judge before, and oh, my fur and whiskers, but wasn't he grand! He walked very slowly, and looked as though he were old enough to be Grandfather Sebastian's grandfather! On his head he wore a great white wig, and he was dressed in scarlet with snowy white lace at his paws. At last he reached his seat and the trial began.

A nasty mouse, dressed in black, with a tiny wig perched on the back of his head, stood up and began to speak.

"Me Lud," he said to the Judge, "you see before you a very wicked mouse by the name of Horace of Holton. On the Tuesday of last week he stole a large piece of rare old cheese from the farm on the corner, the said cheese being the property of Fanny the Farm Mouse."

The old Judge took out a golden snuff box from his pocket, sniffed at the snuff that was inside it, sneezed three times, wiped his face with a purple handkerchief, and mumbled, "Can ye prove it?"

"Yes, me Lud," replied the nasty mouse dressed in black. "Here is Fanny the Farm Mouse to tell you for herself." Whereupon Fanny promised to tell the whole truth and nothing but the truth, and went on to say how she had seen Horace stealing the cheese last Tuesday, at a quarter to ten, in the morning.

The Judge looked very fierce as he said to Horace, "What have you to say for yourself?" But Uncle Horace was very frightened and didn't say anything at all.

It seemed to us that the Judge was going to send him to prison when a strange little mouse suddenly piped up, "It's lies, that's what it is; all lies! Fanny ate the cheese herself; I saw her, and so did my friends." At which a number of mice stood up, nodding their heads hard.

Well, the old Judge was so confused by all this that he didn't know what to say; so he took out his golden snuff box from his pocket, sniffed at the snuff that was inside it, sneezed three times, wiped his face with his purple handkerchief, and glowered at Fanny. But Fanny had given herself away, for she was blushing a bright red colour to the roots of her hair, and the tears were pouring down her cheeks.

"You are very wicked," said the Judge. "You must not bear false witness against your neighbour. Go to prison." Then he turned to the Police Mice; "Let Horace go," he commanded them, "but first give him the biggest piece of cheese that you can find."

GREAT POSSESSIONS

We were all gathered together in Snarford Church one wet evening. Grandfather Sebastian had just enjoyed some of the bits of food which we had brought with us, and so he was in a better mood than usual. "Tell us a story, Grandfather," demanded Freddie, while his young wife, Phoebe of Faldingworth chimed in, "Yes, please do Grandfather dear!" Well, for all his grey hair, his drooping whiskers and his testy manner, Grandfather still has an eye for a pretty face, and Phoebe's face is as pretty as they come! So it was that the old mouse told this tale.

"Once upon a time," he began, "there was a rich young mouse who lived in a farmhouse larder. He had as safe a nest as any mouse could wish to have in a hole beneath the floor boards; he had warmth and comfort, and as much as he wanted to eat! The farmer's wife kept her larder well stocked, and as she was particularly fond of cheese the shelves were piled high with great rounds of country cheeses of every colour and flavour. So," went on Grandfather, "you might have thought that that rich young mouse was very lucky; and yet he was not as happy as he should have been. In spite of there being no cats in the house, nor rats, nor traps; in spite of a nest which was warm and snug; in spite of a tummy which was always full; in spite of all these things he felt that something was missing."

Grandfather paused for a moment to get his breath back, and we waited in silence to hear what it was that the rich young mouse could possibly need. At last he began again.

"One day there came to the farmstead a young mouse whom he had never seen before. The stranger had an odd fascination about him, so that those who heard him speak felt forced to listen carefully to every word that he spoke. The rich young mouse was glad to have a visitor, and was soon showing him around his home, and offering him a choice of Cheddar or Gorgonzola cheese with a biscuit. So attracted was he by the stranger, and so much at ease did he feel with him, that he suddenly blurted out, 'You know, I feel that there is something missing in my life; I wonder what it can be?'

"For a moment the stranger looked into his eyes, as though he was reading his inmost thoughts. Then he spoke very slowly and very quietly, and this is what he said. 'Go, give up your nest to a family of homeless mice, and follow me!'

"The rich young mouse thought long and deeply, he thought of the happiness that would come to that family of homeless mice; he thought of the excitement and joy of following this strange and compelling visitor. Then he looked down at his warm and snug little nest, and he looked up at the great round cheeses. And he turned away sorrowful, for he was one that had great possessions."

AT THE SEASIDE

Last month I went for a holiday to the seaside. And oh, my fur and whiskers, but what fun I had! First there was the sea, and I could hardly believe my eyes when I saw it; and then there were the sands and the donkeys, and of course all the crumbs from people's picnics. But what I liked best was the fun fair; when no one was looking I jumped on to the big wheel, and when it went up I quite thought that I was going to touch the sky!

After that I began to feel hungry and went to see what I could find to eat; presently I managed to get a huge piece of pink cloudy stuff — it was twice as big as I was! I had never seen anything like it before, but I am told that it was called candy floss. It was great fun eating it, but you know I still felt hungry when I had finished, and it wasn't until I happened to find an old bit of cheese that I had had enough. I suppose that candy floss is not enough for us to live by. That we need the important things even if they may seem dull, like old cheese, Cheddar as well as Stilton.

Then I must tell you about the mirrors; perhaps you have seen them in a fun fair? The glass was so bent that when you looked at yourself in them you were all kinds of shapes and sizes; sometimes tall and thin; sometimes short and fat; sometimes bulging out in all the wrong places.

In one mirror I seemed to have such big teeth that I jumped a foot in the air with fright when I saw myself; in another my tail was so long that I couldn't see the end of it! In another my legs were so long and my body so fat that I looked like a sausage on sticks standing there!

Perhaps, like the candy floss, these mirrors have something to tell us. If we look at ourselves in the wrong way we shall not see what we are really like. But if we ask God to help us, then we shall find out if we are kind or unkind, truthful or untruthful, selfish or unselfish.

So I learnt two lessons at the seaside, for the price of one. But after all the excitement it was rather nice to be back home again in my snug little nest in Wickenby Church, even though there are no mirrors at all, no candy floss and only a chunk of very stale cheese!

HOLIDAYS

For Mickie and Minnie in Snelland Church the holidays mean no school for weeks and weeks — day after day when they play for as long as they like. For Aunt Sarah I'm afraid it means weeks and weeks of having Mickie and Minnie at home up to every kind of mischief, and longing for term to begin again! For Sister Lucy a holiday means visiting other mice's Churches, and sniffing in a rather superior sort of way that they are not nearly so neat and tidy as they should be. Uncle Horace goes off for part of his holiday to spend his money on the latest fashion in clothes — if we mice had a Carnaby Street, which we don't, Uncle Horace would always be there. Freddie and I like to go off together exploring new places, and meeting different mice.

When I went to call upon Grandfather Sebastian one day soon after the holidays had begun he did not seem to be at all pleased to see me.

"Go away!" he growled, "I'm very busy." Since the old mouse was lying back in an old and shabby armchair, with a copy of *The Mouse Times* over his face, I was rather surprised that he should call himself busy. He must have read my thoughts, for he went on, "I am busy

recreating myself."

"What do you mean, Grandfather dear?" I asked him.

"Well," said Grandfather impatiently, sitting up and letting the paper fall to his knees, "you must know what recreation means, don't you?"

"Yes," I replied. "It means playing games and having fun."

"Stuff and nonsense!" he snapped. "Recreation means recreating yourself. Now, be off with you, for I cannot spare you any more time."

So I had to leave him, busy recreating himself, lying quite still with his eyes shut and his drooping old white whiskers moving ever so slightly as he breathed.

When I got home, the Rector was in Church, so I asked him, "What does recreation mean?"

"Well William," he said, "it means making a thing again, making it as fresh and good as it was before, and that is what holidays are for. Some people go away to the seaside for their recreation so that when they come home they are no longer tired and stale. Some play games, or garden, or go for long walks."

I told him about Grandfather.

"Yes," he went on, "some just need a good rest."

I hope you all have a good holiday with lots of fun, and that you come back at the end of it fresh and eager to do God's work, at home or at school or wherever you happen to be. But remember that Grandfather Sebastian is a very old mouse, and you are not likely to find much recreation asleep under a copy of the newspaper!

RECTORY BEARS

Sister Lucy came running into my Church last week, and cried out "You'd never believe it!"

"Believe what?" I asked.

"No, I'm sure you wouldn't," she went on.

"Well, I can't say, can I," I replied, "until I know what you're talking about?"

"Well, I'll tell you," she said, "though I'm still sure you won't believe me." Then coming up to me she whispered in my ear, "There are two black bears in the Rectory garden."

Well, how I did laugh! I laughed until the tears ran down my cheeks; and how pink Lucy turned when I told her that they were not bears but dogs — Newfoundland dogs — like the one called Nana in Peter Pan. Of course I have known about them for a long time now, and I know how gentle and friendly they are, but of course they are very big, and even their paws are bigger than I am.

It's an odd thing, that although they are so big, and look so frightening, yet they are not nearly so unfriendly as little Jezebel the Rectory cat. Now she looks so soft and sweet as she lies dozing in the sun, but oh, my goodness me, she's not nearly so soft and sweet as she looks, and woe betide the poor little mouse that tries to play with her! You know it often happens that things that look frightening at first, are really not so bad after all, while things that look all right are really and truly just the opposite!

These two great big dogs, which Lucy thought were black bears, are very friendly and love playing together, and if I asked them I am sure that they would love to play with me. But even though they would mean me no harm they might easily knock me over, and then supposing one of them trod on my tail by mistake! Or supposing they forgot I was a mouse and thought that I was a bit of one of the Rector's socks which they love to chew! They wouldn't mean any harm, but it wouldn't be very comfortable for me, would it?

So it is with lots of things which you will see when you grow up. Things which are good, and nice to enjoy, so long as you enjoy them in the right way; a dish of strawberries and cream — that's lovely so I'm told; but what about twenty dishes one after the other — ugh!

These dogs, and Jezebel have taught me two things, and I hope you will not mind a rather stupid little Church Mouse telling you what they are, because they might help you. First, do not decide that you like or dislike a person or a thing without thinking; if I had done that I might have run away from the dogs and tried to make friends with the cat! And secondly, even if a thing is good, like strawberries and cream, or Cheddar cheese, do not let it rule your life; if I had let those dogs do as they liked with me I might have got squashed — by mistake you understand, but still squashed!

PRUNES

Did you hear the thunder we had soon after Easter, and does thunder frighten you, I wonder? If it makes you jump, then please spare a thought for the poor little Church Mice, because it sounds so much louder to us than it does to you. One night as it was thundering outside, I sat in the doorway to my little home and listened to the rumbling, and watched the walls of the Church being lit up by the bright flashes of lightning; as I did so, I remembered a story which I had once been told.

There was a little boy, and his name was Jimmie. Once he was given prunes and custard for dinner; now Jimmie was not very fussy about his food, but if there was one thing that he could not abide, then that one thing was — prunes! His mother knew this, and so she had given him a large bowl of custard, which he loved, with just two of the detested prunes swimming in the middle of it.

Well, Jimmie had soon eaten all the custard, but the two prunes were left stranded high and dry, at the bottom of his plate.

"Now then, come along Jimmie dear, eat them up," said his mother briskly.

"I don't like prunes," he muttered.

"Never mind that," said his mother rather more sharply, "eat them up quickly."

But Jimmie only just sat there, and said, "I don't like prunes, and I won't eat them." At this his mother became very cross.

"You're a naughty little boy," she scolded, "go to your room. God will be very angry with you." And so Jimmie went off to his room.

Soon after he had gone a thunderstorm broke over their house, and his mother began to wonder if he would be frightened up there alone in his room; so she hurried upstairs, and peeped round the door. By now the storm was at its worst, and there were great loud crashes of thunder, and blinding flashes of lightning. Jimmie was standing by the open window, looking out at the furious raging of the storm, his eyes open wide with wonder; then between the crashes of thunder his mother heard him speak.

"Oh God," he said, "what a fuss to make over two prunes!"

Now I am sure that there must be a lesson to be learnt from this, but quite honestly I don't know what it is! Certainly the boy was naughty not to eat his prunes, but I think that his mother was really very silly, telling him that God would be angry with him. What do you think?

UNCLEAN

Uncle Horace came into my Church last Wednesday and at once I knew that something was wrong.

"What is it Uncle Horace?" I asked, for he really did look very cross, and usually he is so cheerful.

"Why, young William me lad," he said, trying to sound as bright as usual but not really succeeding, "it seems to me most unfair. I was having a peep in the Bible, near the beginning of it in a book called Leviticus, and do you know what I read there?" I shook my head, and so he went on.

"It said," spluttered Uncle Horace, looking as angry as his round face and purple-coloured waistcoat would let him look, "it said, 'There shall be unclean unto you among the creeping things that creep upon the earth; the weasel, and the mouse, and the tortoise after his kind, and the ferret, and the chameleon, and the lizard, and the snail, and the mole.' And you know," he continued, "that unclean here means bad and nasty!"

Well I must say it did seem to be very unfair. Of course the weasel is

bad, and the ferret is nasty, and the chameleon is an old turncoat, and the lizard and the snail — ugh! And the tortoise is a lazy good-for-nothing, and the mole is so very black. But a mouse — whoever heard of a mouse being bad and nasty?

"I tell you what," said Uncle Horace in his usual impulsive way, "we'll go straight round to Grandfather Sebastian and see what he has to say about it." So off we hurried along the road to Snarford, and as we went he kept on muttering away to himself, "Mice unclean, whatever next? Mice bad and nasty? Oh, my fur and whiskers!"

Grandfather had evidently been having a snooze and did not seem very pleased to see us.

"Well, Horace and William, what do you want?" he mumbled at us, and Uncle Horace told him.

"There now," he exclaimed, "doesn't that make you see red?"

With a frown on his brow, but a twinkle in his eye Grandfather replied, "I can only see purple when I look at your waistcoat Horace, why don't you dress like a proper Church Mouse?"

"Never mind my clothes Grandfather," said Horace, "what do you think of mice being called unclean, and nasty and bad, in the Bible?"

"Well," said Grandfather slowly after a moment's thought, "I don't think that I mind very much. That was written a very long time ago, and I am sure that God doesn't think of us as unclean or nasty. When you get home, you read how God loves all his creatures, even though He may not mention each one by name. You read Psalm 84, verses 3 and 4." And with that the fierce old mouse made it quite obvious that he wanted us to go, grumbling away under his breath about there being no peace and quiet these days.

When we got back to Wickenby we read Grandfather's verses, and this is what they said:

'Yea, the sparrow hath found her an house, and the swallow a nest for herself, where she may lay her young, even thine altars, O Lord of hosts, my King, and my God.'

FOUNDATIONS

Jesus once told a story about two houses. One was built on a rock, and no matter how fiercely the wind blew against it, it could not blow the house down. The other was built on sand, and when the storms came and the wind blew, that house fell down and, said Jesus, "Great was the fall of it." Now I am only a little mouse and not very clever, but I know what Jesus meant. He meant that if you build your life upon a trust in Him, then when difficulties and sorrows and temptations blow against it your trust will remain, and your life will not be really spoilt. But if you build your life upon a trust in anything other than God, then when difficulties and sorrows and temptations come, they will be more than you can bear.

I was reminded of this story one Saturday last month; it was very early in the morning, and it happened like this.

It was a wild night, the wind was howling around the Church, and I was thankful that I was snug in my warm little hole under the floor. Louder and louder the gale blew, the branches of the trees creaked and groaned, the pigeons in the Church tower fluttered uneasily from nest to nest, and I wondered how my poor cousins the Harvest Mice were faring out on a night like that. They had moved, so I heard, from their nest which they expected the big combine to knock down, and had moved to some ivy around the trunk of a great elm tree at the edge of their field.

Then suddenly — there was a sound which made me jump right off the ground with fright. It was a great crash which echoed through the Church and sent me diving into bed, where I pulled the blankets of leaves and paper over my head, and pretended I wasn't there!

For what seemed like ages I lay there as the wind continued to rage above me, but in the end it began to die away, and once again the Church seemed quiet and peaceful. "I wonder if I dare go out to see what made that noise?" I asked myself.

Just then however I heard a scratching on the floor above, and a frightened little voice called down, "May we come in, please?" I knew the voice, and ran up quickly to welcome my cousins the Harvest Mice.

"Oh, you poor things!" I exclaimed, for there they were, Mr and Mrs Harvest Mouse, and their four little boys and two little girls, soaked to the skin and trembling with fright. "Why, whatever has happened?"

As I was busy making them warm and comfortable, and running in and out of my larder with bits of my best cheese for them to eat, they told me all about it.

"You know," they began, "that we moved to the old elm tree; well suddenly when the wind was at its fiercest, and with no warning at all, there was a noise like a gun going off, and it came crashing down to the ground."

"I heard the noise," I joined in, "but I never dreamt that it was your tree that made it."

"Well," squeaked Mrs Harvest Mouse, "we should have known better. Was it not our old enemy Mr Owl who once said, 'Never trust an elm tree — it's as dangerous as a house built on sand'?"

CHEASLES

Aunt Sarah's children, Mickie and Minnie, were walking home from school a few weeks ago when Minnie suddenly stopped, stared hard at Mickie, and said, "Why! Whatever are all those spots on your face?"

"What spots?" asked Mickie. "I haven't got any spots."

"Oh yes you have," his sister retorted, "and oh my! You do look funny!"

Mickie, who was a bit cross because he wasn't feeling very well, sniffed with disgust and hurried on home to Snelland Church.

As soon as Aunt Sarah saw him she exclaimed, "Mickie! What are all those red spots on your face?"

Minnie giggled with delight as she whispered, "There you are, I told you so!"

In no time at all Aunt Sarah had Mickie out of his clothes, and then even he could see that he was indeed covered all over with bright red spots! "Do you know," said Aunt Sarah, "I do believe that you've got the cheasles!"

Well, the next morning Doctor Mouse came to see Mickie; he took his temperature, looked at his spots, and soon confirmed what Aunt Sarah had said.

"Yes, my lad, you've got cheasles all right," he declared, "you must stay here quietly until all the spots have gone."

Silly Minnie thought it was terribly funny. "Mickie," she cried, "you look just like a red currant bun!" And oh, my fur and whiskers, how cross he was with her! But she stopped laughing some days later when she caught the cheasles, and looked like a red currant bun herself; then it was Mickie's turn to laugh.

"You must be very careful to keep away from other young mice," Doctor Mouse had said, "for cheasles is very catching. It's as catching as a bad habit." When he had gone Mickie and Minnie asked Aunt Sarah to explain what he had meant.

"Why did he say that cheasles is catching, like a bad habit?" they asked.

"Well," said their mother, "you know how easy it is to copy someone else who is unkind, or who boasts, or who tells lies; that is catching a bad habit, and it's best to keep away from those kind of mice for that very reason; and so it is easy to catch the cheasles, and that is why Doctor Mouse told you not to mix with other young mice just now."

One evening Grandfather Sebastian came to see how they were getting on, but Aunt Sarah would not let him come even into the Church.

When he had gone away Mickie said, "But Grandfather is not a young mouse; he couldn't catch it, could he?"

"When grown up mice catch a bad habit — or cheasles," replied Aunt Sarah, "it can be much worse than for little mice, and much more difficult to cure."

As you may imagine, this gave those two pickles, Mickie and Minnie, something really serious to think about as they went to bed that night. Then, just as they were falling asleep Minnie murmured across their nest to Mickie, "Mickie, do you think that good habits are catching too?"

"I don't know," came the sleepy reply; "you can't catch good health can you? You can't catch *not* having cheasles, can you? But somehow I guess you can catch a good habit. Good-night Minnie."

But Minnie was already fast asleep in a land, not of cheasles, but of lovely cheese!

THE HIPPY MOUSE

The other night I was sitting in my hole thinking very hard about — nothing in particular, when I heard a voice calling out in the Church above me. "Hi man!" it said.

When I popped my head outside the most extraordinary sight met my eyes. It was I suppose what you would call a Hippy Mouse, though whether it were a boy or girl mouse I had no idea.

"Hi, man!" it repeated.

"Hi, man!" I replied feeling rather foolish as I did so, but imagining that this was the polite way to address a Hippy Mouse.

It was dressed in green from tip to toe, at least not quite, for its paws were bare and its claws were painted a bright silver. On its face were a pair of large dark glasses, and the long hair on its head was rusty red in colour. As it moved it had to be careful not to trip over the beads which it wore around its neck; row upon row of them, and I rather fancy that they were grape stones strung together.

"Would you care for a little something to eat?" I asked.

"Is that your pad, man?" it enquired pointing to my nest, and

followed me down. When we were enjoying a piece of old cheese I asked what its name was.

"Why, don't you know?" it said surprised, "I'm Lynn, man, from the farm."

Well, I would never have known, but of course I didn't say so, and merely murmured, "Of course. Have some more cheese." Lynn's red hair and silver claws had not spoilt her appetite, and for a while we ate in silence. Then suddenly she spoke again.

"I have a surprise."

"Oh," I replied rather nervously, "what is it?"

"Go up into the Church man," she said, "and see for yourself."

At first I saw nothing unusual, and then there they were! On the Altar step four of the most unusual mice you ever did see. Like Lynn they were bare pawed, but instead of green, each wore purple jeans and an orange shirt. On the end of their noses they wore steel-rimmed glasses, and the hair on their heads was very long. In their paws they each held a guitar, about the size of a new penny piece.

Lynn seemed to go into a kind of trance as she stared at them, "Groovy man, groovy!" she kept on muttering.

"Why, whoever are they?" I demanded. "And what are they doing in my Church, and on the Altar step too?"

"Why man," she exclaimed, "they're Nicky and the Nibblers!"

As she spoke they began, as she put it, 'to do their thing'. They shouted and they screamed; they twisted and they turned; and they strummed away for all they were worth on their guitars. Lynn said it was a hippy hymn, but to me it sounded hellish! Quite suddenly it was all over and they were making for the door, with Lynn hard at their heels.

"Must take some bread to a poor mouse down the lane," she called out, "be seeing you, man."

When the old Church was quiet again, and still, and sleepy, I crept up to the Altar step, fearful and ashamed. There in the stained glass window was Jesus looking down at me, Jesus who had once whipped some Jews out of the Temple because they did not treat it with proper respect.

"I'm sorry, Lord," I whispered, "don't be too angry, for they meant well." And do you know, I could have sworn that the Lord smiled down at me.

"Angry?" I heard Him chuckle. "It was heavenly . . . man!"

ANTS

We once knew a very inquisitive little mouse called Jeremy. As well as being inquisitive, some of us believed that he could perform magic, as you are about to hear.

One day, when Jeremy was visiting my Church, we saw an anthill in the Churchyard. We watched closely as two ants ran along the ground and into the hill.

"I wonder what kind of life they lead in there?" murmured Jeremy. "And how many of them there are; and what they talk about; and what they have for their tea?"

"You'll never know, will you?" and I laughed as I added, "unless you turn yourself into an ant and go in there with them!"

No sooner had I spoken than Jeremy had completely vanished away! There was nowhere he could have hidden and yet — he simply wasn't there!

"William!" squeaked a familiar voice at my paws, and I got such a fright that I jumped clean off the ground! I looked round again but the only sign of life was a tiny ant. "Do be careful," it snapped crossly, "you

nearly trod on me."

Oh my, oh my! Oh my fur and whiskers! But do you know, Jeremy had changed into an ant!

"I'm going into this hill," he called out, "to find out all I can about these ants," and with that, in he went.

For a long time I waited there, and then just as I was saying to myself, "William, you've been dreaming!" there was Jeremy, no longer an ant, but a mouse once more.

"I've had such an interesting time," he told me, "and one day I'll tell you all about it."

When I told the family, how they laughed!

"Oh William," spluttered Uncle Horace with the tears running down his cheeks, "you must be going soft in the head!" But they all became quite quiet when Grandfather Sebastian began to speak.

"I don't know," he said slowly. "It's not the first time that something like this has happened."

"Tell us, Grandfather," we urged.

"It was a long, long time ago," he went on, "that God looked down from heaven into this world of ours, and wondered to Himself what it would be like to be a man, and said 'I'll become a man myself, and then I'll find out.' Of course before He could become a man, He had to become a baby, and be born in Bethlehem. But that Baby in Bethlehem was really none other than God Himself. He had come to discover what people are like, what makes them happy or sad; what they like and what they don't like; even what they have for tea!"

Afterwards I thought about what Grandfather had said; about God coming into the world on the first Christmas Day to find out all about people, and who knows, little Church Mice too! But I still sometimes wonder if Jeremy's magic had been a dream!

HOT LINE TO GOD

Perhaps you think that Church Mice find it easy to pray, but you would be wrong. It is true that we join in from our places under your pews when you are saying the Lord's Prayer. But we find it hard to think what we are saying, and if I am alone in my nest I find it hard to pray at all; in fact sometimes I say a prayer without even thinking what it means!

My cousin Jack the Ship's Mouse, travels as far as my dear friends the swallows, to tropical lands beyond the seas. He once told me of some sailors who had the most wonderful pet bird; it was bright red and blue in colour and it talked! It would say, "Pretty Polly," and, "Good-morning," and part of the Lord's Prayer! But some of its sayings would have made poor Sister Lucy blush!

"It must have been a very wise bird," I said.

"Well, not really," Jack replied. "You see it didn't understand what it said. It would say 'Good-night' at breakfast-time, and sometimes the words of the Lord's Prayer got terribly mixed up. And as to the bad language, I don't believe he understood a word of it — any more than I did!" he added hastily.

Well I find sometimes that I am saying my prayers rather like that parrot, repeating them by heart and not thinking what they mean. One morning the words simply wouldn't come, and I felt a long, long way from God; I couldn't see Him, and I didn't know what to say, so instead I went for a stroll outside.

There in the Churchyard sitting on a telephone wire, was the very oddest looking bird you ever did see. Could it be a parrot? I wondered excitedly, but no, it was even odder than a parrot.

"Hello!" I called up. "What is your name?"

"Busby," he called down, and as he spoke he laughed so much that he nearly fell off the wire. When he had smoothed down his feathers, he spluttered out between more chuckles, "Why haven't you got a telephone in your Church? Then you could talk to God through it."

"Could I?" I called back, "could I see Him through it?"

"Well no, of course you couldn't!" and he burst out laughing so much at the idea of seeing God through the telephone that this time he did fall off the wire; it was only after a great deal of flapping and squawking that he regained his perch.

"Well, if I had a telephone, would it tell me what to say?" However this idea left poor Busby quite incapable of saying anything at all, as he

sat there, shaking with laughter. But then quite suddenly his mood changed, and he fluttered down to the ground beside me.

"I tell you what, little mouse," he said quietly, "you pretend you have a telephone, a new video-phone I think they call it. Pretend that you can hear God talking to you, and that you can see his kind face. Then you will begin to enjoy talking with Him so much that you won't want to stop." At that he began to chuckle again.

"And I'll tell you another thing little mouse — you won't even have a telephone bill to pay!"

The thought of a *free* service to God made him turn three somersaults in the air, and to loop the loop as he disappeared over the trees.

WARNINGS

Champion, the Rectory Wonder Pony, is so fat and lazy that sometimes he walks slowly across the grass and thinks, and sometimes he just thinks. Although there was once a boy, so I am told, that saw him trot, but that was a very long time ago.

So you may find it hard to believe what I saw last week. The Rectory Mouse had taken me to say good-afternoon to Champion who was walking slowly towards us when he brushed against a new red wire, with his nose. And then . . . . Oh my fur and whiskers but then! did you ever see such a sight in your life! That fat, lazy pony jumped back two whole yards and galloped off! Yes actually galloped! Round and round the garden he went, and every now and then he jumped right up in the air with all four feet off the ground! At last he slowed down and came towards us, but as soon as he saw that new red wire he was off again, bucking and rearing, and looking every bit like Champion the real Wonder Horse.

When we had finished laughing — and oh dearie, dearie me, how we did laugh, the Rectory Mouse managed to explain.

"It's an electric fence."

"Well," I replied, "I think it's very unkind putting up a horrid thing like that." But the Rectory Mouse didn't agree.

"No, it's not unkind. Without that wire he might easily run away and get lost, or perhaps be hurt by a passing car." And she went on with a chuckle. "After all, he won't touch it again!"

Later we went indoors to enjoy some of the Rector's cheese, when she said, "There are lots of things like that wire you know."

"Are there?" I asked, for I had never seen anything like it, and neither had Champion, I thought to myself!

"There's a holly leaf," she said, "that has sharp points which say 'Don't touch me or I will prick you!' Or a soft 'Miaow' which says 'Keep very still or else!' Or a little voice inside you which says 'Do this, because it's right; or don't do that, because it's wrong.' "

A few days later another funny thing happened. I went to see the Rectory Mouse again, and as we walked down the garden she said, "That wire is switched off today, and wouldn't hurt anyone."

But do you think Champion would go near it? No, not he!

HEAVEN

What a lovely Harvest Supper we had at Holton, and how glad I was that Uncle Horace invited me to go! Home-made bread there was, and soup, and tongue, and ham, and lovely apple pie, and cheese and biscuits. All quite free too — for us Church Mice that is!

"Oh my!" Uncle Horace kept on muttering to himself, "this is heavenly, absolutely heavenly!" And the more he kept on saying "This is heavenly!" the more he ate. And the more he ate the more he kept on muttering, "Heavenly! Yes, absolutely heavenly!" Well, perhaps it did seem heavenly at the time, but that night when he was back in his nest in Holton Church I am sorry to say that Uncle Horace did not feel at all well! In fact he felt very, very ill, and all that night his poor little tummy kept on saying to him, "Oh Horace, how could you be so greedy?"

"Heavenly!" he had called all those good things, but I am sure that heaven does not just mean apple pie, even for a very hungry little Church Mouse. Nor does it mean a huge saucer of milk for Jezebel the cat, nor large and luscious bones for those Rectory dogs. Nor for that matter should heaven mean just chocolates and ice-cream for a boy or

girl. I had a good idea of what heaven should not mean, but just what it should mean I really had no idea at all, until some days later when there was a Harvest Service in Snarford.

The whole family went there except Uncle Horace who had not fully recovered from his night out. Now there was a time when Grandfather Sebastian hated anyone disturbing his peace on a Sunday morning, but he doesn't seem to mind so much now, though he does still grumble a bit; "No peace at all," he will say, "what do they think they're doing?" But he doesn't really mean it — at least I don't think that he does!

Anyway, when the Service was over he asked where Uncle Horace was. "Buying himself some more fancy clothes, I suppose," he grumbled, "instead of coming to see a poor lonely old mouse!" I didn't remind him how much he dislikes having to meet Uncle Horace, but instead told him all about the apple pies, and how he kept on calling them heavenly.

"What is heaven like, Grandfather?" I asked.

For a moment his eyes twinkled, "Heaven is where I can have some rare old Gorgonzola cheese, and not have to answer stupid questions from little mice!"

"But Grandfather," I protested, "surely that is not a stupid question."

"No, young William," he went on slowly, "it is not a stupid question, but it is a very hard one to answer. We know that heaven is where God is, because Jesus told us to pray to 'Our Father which art in heaven.' " He stopped for a moment, and then went on. "What makes it all so difficult is that we will talk about heaven as a place, as though we could go there in an aeroplane; but really it is not a place at all."

"If it's not a place what is it?" I asked. There was another pause, so long this time that I thought the old mouse had dropped off to sleep. At last however, he began to pull at his long grey whiskers, and this is what he said:

"Heaven is being with God, doing the kind of things that God wants us to do, and enjoying doing them. In heaven we shall be happy because we are close to God, and because the things that make Him happy will make us happy too. He will love us, just as He does now, but we shall love Him too. It is a way of living, and has nothing whatever to do with a place."

'Nor with apple pie?' I thought to myself rather wistfully!

HARVEST MICE

You are learning to do all sorts of things that I will never be able to do, and wouldn't want to anyway! If I were a boy I should learn my sums, and how to play football, and lots of other things, but it really would be rather funny if we Church Mice had to do sums and play football; though of course we do have to learn how to write, else how could I be writing these stories for you?

Then of course we learn to do things that you could never do; you couldn't jump through a tiny hole in the floor could you? Nor live quite happily for a week on a little bit of cheese! Last week I did something that I would never have thought possible; I had tea on the top of a stalk of corn, and it happened like this.

A little country cousin of mine, a Harvest Mouse, popped into my Church.

"Hallo," she squeaked, "we were wondering if you would like to come to tea with us before we move."

"Why, yes please," I replied, for I never refuse an invitation to tea.

"Oh, good, come along with me now then, for there is not too much time."

Together we ran down the Church path, through the gate, over the road, and into the field. I would soon have got lost, for all around me towered the great tall stalks of corn; but my little friend took me by the paw and led me along a twisting lane for what seemed a very long way; how she ever found her house I shall never know, but find it she did. What a funny sight it was hung there before my eyes, and I say hung because it did hang from the tops of several stalks of corn, swaying gently in the breeze. We ran up one of those stalks and into the nest at the top of it.

Inside were her children, four litle boys and two girls who each said, "How do you do?" most politely. For tea we had grains of corn, of which there were plenty, as you may guess, being in the middle of a cornfield. I rather wished that there were some crumbs of bread and a little bit of cheese, but of course I would not have said so for the world!

"It's harvest time," they told me; "soon the farmer will come and cut down our home, and before then we must move to safety." I should never have thought of this, nor would I have known how to make so snug a nest as theirs, on the top of some corn, in the middle of a field.

"When the food becomes hard to find," I told them, "and when the cold winter weather comes, you must come to stay with me; I'll save you some corn from the Harvest Festival." Gladly they promised that they would indeed come.

When we had finished, they showed me the way out of the cornfield, and we said goodbye at the side of the road. As I wandered up the Churchyard path I thought to myself, 'What a wonderful thing it is, that God should help us all, creatures great and small, to make our homes in our own way, and to find food for ourselves and our children, and that He should find time to watch over even the tiniest of us.'

AN IMP

"Tell us a story, Grandfather, about when you were a young mouse," said young Mickie. Well, Grandfather had enjoyed so much Stilton cheese that his head was beginning to nod, but like all old mice he does enjoy talking about the long ago.

"I remember," he began, and we all settled back to listen. "I remember when I was a very young mouse I lived in the Cathedral, and had a comfortable nest under the Shrine of St. Hugh. Our family had lived there for hundreds of years and during all that time stories had been handed down from old mice to their children and grandchildren so that the stories were as old as the Cathedral itself.

"One story," he went on, "was that when St. Hugh built his Choir some Angels came and made their home in it, living up close to the roof and adding the music of their harps and trumpets to the singing of the men and boys so far beneath them. Then one day who should come running into the Cathedral but a bad little imp! Oh, my fur and whiskers, but wasn't he bad!" And Grandfather glowered at young Mickie, as much as to say, 'Almost as bad as you!'

"What a lot of mischief he got up to, painting horrid pictures on the walls, breaking the candles, and even putting drawing pins on the Bishop's throne!"

"Oooh!" gasped Mickie and Minnie with delighted disbelief!

"Aah!" exclaimed Sister Lucy with disgust, while I'm afraid to say that Uncle Horace gave a loud guffaw!

However, Grandfather heard none of this for he was six hundred years away, back in the days of St. Hugh as he went on with his story.

" 'Let's turn the rascal out,' exclaimed a rather stern Angel.

" 'Oh must we?' pleaded a Boy Angel who had secretly longed to do something of the sort himself! And so the Angels had a great discussion and in the end they decided that he might stay 'where we can keep an eye on him' as they put it, but really because they were too kind to send him away. 'After all,' said the Boy Angel, 'this is *His* Father's house as well as ours.'

"Today," said Grandfather, "if you go to the Cathedral you will still see those Angels up above the Choir, and if you look very carefully, you will see the imp hiding amongst some carvings on a pillar.

"So Mickie," the old mouse concluded, "when you hear the stories of the Christmas Angels, think of those Angels and the imp who share our lovely Cathedral because God loves His imps as much as He loves His Angels."

The story was over, and as Mickie and Minnie played noisily around the Church the Stilton cheese seemed to be saying to Grandfather "Go to sleep . . . sleep . . . " The last we heard as the old grey head gave a final nod was a whisper, "God and His Angels must be much more patient than I could ever be!"

THE ARTIST MOUSE

One hot summer's day an old mouse sat in the middle of a field, looking puzzled. His name was Arthur and he called himself the Artist Mouse because he thought that he was good at painting — which was more than his family did!

As he sat there a little friend of his came along blowing a merry tune on her penny whistle.

"Hallo!" she cried out, "why do you look so sad?"

"Because," he replied, "I want to paint some clouds and there is not a cloud in the sky!"

"Never mind," she replied cheerily, "I'll tell you what to do. Go and sit under that bush, hang some balls of cotton wool on it, and paint them. They will look just like clouds in the sky!"

Well Arthur is not only an artistic mouse, he is also a trusting one, and he said to himself, "If that's what she suggests, that's what I'll do." So he found some bits of cotton wool, and after some difficulty hung them on the bush.

"There now," his friend said, "whenever you want advice, just ask

me," and off she scampered, still playing on her whistle.

Arthur sat down, got out his paints, and very carefully copied the little bits of cotton wool hanging on the bush. But when he had finished and looked at his picture, a tear ran slowly down his poor old cheek; for do you know what he saw instead of the clouds for which he had hoped? — Some little bits of cotton wool hanging on a bush!

After a few moments he stopped being sad and became very cross instead.

"What a stupid little mouse she is," he said to himself. "She may be good at playing her penny whistle but her ideas on painting are no help at all!"

That night he came to supper, and told us all of what had happened.

"We know her well," said Freddie, "she is really a very silly little mouse!"

"And flighty too!" put in Phoebe. Then Grandfather began to speak.

"I have never had time to waste on painting; but if I wished to paint a cloud I would not paint some balls of cotton wool, just because some young flibbertigibbet of a mouse told me to do so!" Then in a gentler voice he went on, "I'll give you a harder task than painting clouds that are not there. Paint me a picture of God!"

Arthur thought for a moment. "Shall I paint an old man above the sky? Or a king on his golden throne? Shall I paint a great warrior, or a man full of learning? Or the beauty of a sunset? Or the power of a thunderstorm?" Then he got out his paints, and he painted a simple picture of a poor young Man hanging on a Cross. "That's God," he said.

JACK THE SAILOR MOUSE

The other day I was enjoying forty winks after my dinner when I was suddenly awakened by a loud cry of, "Ahoy there! Anyone aboard?" I got up quickly and peeped out from my hole, and there by the door stood my long lost cousin, Jack the Sailor Mouse!

He was wearing a blue roll-neck jersey, and had a sailor's hat perched on the back of his head. When he saw me peeping out from my hole, he came across the Church, and as he came he rolled from side to side like a ship at sea.

"Well, well, well, my hearty," he shouted as he held out a paw, "shiver me timbers, but it's a long time since we met; and how's my old Church Mouse after all these years?"

In no time at all I had him down in my little home, and was plying him with the best food that I could find in my larder. When he could eat no more, he settled back and began to tell me tales of the sea, and of his wonderful adventures. He told of great voyages to the four corners of the earth; of calm nights under a tropical sky; of storms and tempests, and of ships laden with cheese. I almost thought I was at sea myself, he talked so much.

"One thing I learnt," he said, "I learnt never to move far without my lifebelt. At one time I didn't bother, but then one night in the Indian Ocean a sudden storm hit the ship, and she heeled over and began to sink. I was a raw young Sailor Mouse then, and while the wise old hands were kept afloat by their lifebelts as they swam across to various packing cases, I was at the very point of drowning when I was hauled to safety by some of my mates. How cross they were at my stupidity!"

Well, Jack the Sailor Mouse agreed to spend his leave with me, and many a yarn did he spin. Then one morning we saw a lot of children coming in for Sunday-school.

"Let's go up, and hear what's going on," I suggested, and made to clamber out of the hole.

"Avast there!" he shouted, "I'm for staying between decks. No Sunday-school or Church for me; I'm a mouse of the world, ye see!"

And so it was that while Jack stayed down below, I sat in my usual place to listen and to join in where I could. The last hymn was one of my favourites, 'Loving Shepherd of Thy sheep, keep Thy lamb in safety keep'. When it was over I went on sitting there, thinking of Jesus, the Good Shepherd, who cares for His sheep, and keeps His lambs and His children, and even little mice like us. Afterwards I went down to my nest and found Jack sitting there, very quietly for once.

"You know," he said, "I couldn't help hearing that last hymn. If Jesus really keeps His children in safety, he must be almost like a lifebelt. Perhaps I should think more of Him than I have done, for fear that one day I may need Him as I once needed that lifebelt."

Of course he was right, but I think that there is a lot more to it than that, don't you? We should love God, not only because He will keep us from harm, but because He first loved us.

I SAW A LITTLE MOUSE

A cat once said to himself, "I wish I could see the Queen!" And then he asked himself, "Why shouldn't I?" And then he told himself, "I will!" So he set off on the long journey to London Town. After many adventures he found himself, one afternoon, outside Buckingham Palace, and when the sentries weren't looking, he slipped in through the great big doors, and ran along miles of red carpets until at last he came to the room where the Queen was having tea.

"Oh my!" he miaowed to himself, "I really am going to see the Queen!" When a footman, dressed in scarlet and gold went in with a plate of hot crumpets, the cat slipped in after him; and then, what do you think happened? Sure enough the Queen was there, having her second cup of tea, but the cat never saw her — all he saw was a little mouse under her chair! At once he forgot all about the Queen and chased the mouse across the room!

Can you picture the scene? The cat chasing the mouse, and the footman chasing the cat, dropping hot crumpets all over the carpet as he went! The Queen, of course, was very brave, and went on drinking tea, though she must have been very sad about those hot crumpets. Her maid screamed, jumped on to a table and upset all the royal strawberry jam! In the excitement the mouse escaped from the cat, and the cat escaped from the footman, but when he was safely outside, the cat remembered that he had never seen the Queen!

I don't live in Buckingham Palace, but in my dear old Church, and I have never seen the Queen; however this story makes me think of people who come to Church to be with God, and who never see Him. Jesus knew that when He went back to Heaven he would find it difficult to picture Him, or to come close to Him. So on the night before he died He had a farewell supper with His friends, and told us that when we remember that Supper in our Communion Service we would remember Him.

When you are confirmed and take part in the Communion Service, be sure to see through the bread and wine to Jesus Himself, who will be there just as He was at that Last Supper. Don't be like that cat who never saw what he had gone to see!

Pussy cat, pussy cat, where have you been?
I've been to London to see the Queen.
Pussy cat, pussy cat, what saw you there?
I saw a little mouse under her chair!

CHEESE IN THE SKY

I went to tea with my Aunt Sarah in Snelland Church a week or two ago. It was always fun going there because you get a good old nursery tea with plenty to eat. My young cousins, Mickie and Minnie were singing nursery rhymes when I arrived, and were running in and out of the pulpit shouting:

"Hey! diddle-diddle,
The cat and fiddle,
The cow jumped over the moon;
The little dog laughed to see such fun,
While the dish ran away with the spoon."

"I don't know about a cow jumping over the moon," I laughed, "but I do know that a little mouse was sent up into space, flying around in a space suit, long before men dared to go up there; perhaps a mouse will land on the moon one day, and that would be fun for him, because they do say that the moon is made of cheese, and oh my, but what a feast he

could have! Fancy having the moon for your dinner!"

"Don't talk such nonsense to the children!" said Aunt Sarah, "why, whatever will you think of next? When I see the moon," she went on, "I like to think about it in the same way as St. Francis did. When the kind saint who loved all God's creatures was near the end of his life, he sang a wonderful song, part of which went like this: 'Praised be my Lord for our sister the moon, and for the stars, the which He has set clear and lovely in heaven.' "

"Yes, of course," I said, "I was only joking, and what you say is very true."

It was dark as I set off on my long walk home, and up in the sky was a great round moon. As I trudged along I thought to myself 'What a wonderful person God must be, that He can set our sister moon up there, and all the stars, and that He still has time to watch over a little mouse like me, wending his way homeward along a country lane.'

I am afraid that the moon up there in the sky still reminded me of a huge round cheese, and the more I looked at it the hungrier I got. I soon forgot all about what Aunt Sarah had said, and about God, and St. Francis, and could think only of a wonderful life in which there was nothing to do but nibble from the biggest cheese you ever saw!

However, that night when I was safely tucked up in my nest I did think about these things again, and I hope you will too; about how wonderful God must be, who has made this world of ours, and the sun, and the moon, and the stars, and more stars beyond the farthest stars that we can see; and who yet can care for a little mouse like me, or a little child like you.

WHAT A GOOD MOUSE AM I!

You will know, I expect, that people come from far away to see our Churches. But perhaps you don't know that many birds and animals come as well. Some of them, like the swallows, even come from away across the sea.

One day a party of mice arrived in the porch of my Church here in Wickenby, and asked if they might look around.

"Why of course!" I exclaimed, "come along in!"

For a time we walked around the Church and I showed them things of interest, such as the hole where I keep my winter's supply of food, and the hole that is ready for me to bolt down should Jezebel the Rectory cat come slinking in. Then we went down to my little home and I offered them what refreshments I had.

As we came out again into the Church, I noticed one of the visitors slip away by himself; he scurried along behind a pew, and then knelt down quietly in a dark corner.

Then one of the others suddenly announced, "I am going to pray!" I cannot say that I really took to him very much; he was larger than the rest, and fatter, and he had a golden watch chain which glistened over his velvety waistcoat; he spoke with a loud, rich fruity sort of voice, in a rather condescending manner, as though he had got mixed up with a party of little Church Mice by mistake, and should really have been in much grander company.

We all watched in silence as he strutted slowly up the aisle. When he reached the choir step he stopped and peeped round, just to make sure that we were all watching and listening. Then he turned round again to face the altar, and began to address God as one might address a public meeting, in a loud voice which demanded attention.

"God," he proclaimed, "I thank Thee that I am not as other mice are — especially these miserable little Church Mice! I say my prayers every day, I give away a tenth of all my cheese, and I am indeed a good and worthy mouse, O God!"

When he had finished and all was quiet once more, I ran along to where the other little mouse had gone to a dark corner behind a pew. He was a poor thing, and no watch chain glistened on his threadbare waistcoat.

"God," he was whispering so softly that I could scarcely hear what he said, "God be merciful to me, a sinner!"

I didn't tell the others what I had heard, and soon, after many goodbyes, they were gone.

Sometimes as I lie in my nest at night-time, I almost believe that I can hear God speaking to me. That night as I lay in the silence of my dear old Church I did hear a still, small voice murmuring in my ear, and this is what it seemed to say:

"William, it was the timid little mouse that pleased me most — much more than the one who was showing off."

TOOTHACHE

Going to the dentist is rather like saying sorry, it's often not as bad as you think it's going to be! You will know that Aunt Sarah has two children, Mickie and Minnie, who live with her in Snelland Church. Well, last week Mickie couldn't eat his dinner, even though it was Cheddar cheese from the Rectory, and so Aunt Sarah asked him what was wrong.

"It's my teeth," he replied, "one of them hurts."

"Well," said Aunt Sarah briskly, "you must go to the dentist."

"Oh, no!" Mickie replied quickly, "I don't think it's as bad as that, in fact I think it's better already!"

When tea-time came, Mickie would not eat his biscuits and complained that they were stale, but Minnie laughed. "They're not, it's your toothache!" So it came about that Mickie was dragged off, much against his will, to the Dentist Mouse.

Aunt Sarah and her reluctant son set off down the road, over the stream, and into the farmyard where the Dentist Mouse lived under the floor of the barn. A lady mouse in a white overall let them in, and Mickie found himself in a big room where there were three other mice

waiting their turn to see the dentist. He amused himself by looking at picture papers and reading the advertisements of very grand mouse-holes for sale.

At last it was his turn, and he was shown into the surgery where an old white mouse took him by the paw, and sat him down in a funny chair that went up and down, and round and about. The white mouse looked in Mickie's mouth and said, "Mmm," and then he looked again and said "Ah-ha." He took a tiny little drill and made it buzz away against Mickie's sore tooth, and then he put some stuff into the hole and said, "Well now, that's all over!"

As Mickie was going out of the room, the white mouse gave him a little parcel for being so good, and when he opened it what do you think he found? Some of his favourite Cheddar cheese and — a delicious piece of apple!

All the way home he kept saying to Aunt Sarah, "When can I go to the Dentist Mouse again?"

If we have toothache we have to go to the dentist or else the pain will get worse; we may not want to go, but we shall be glad when we have been. In the same way when we have hurt someone we have to say sorry, even though we may not want to, but we will be glad when we have done so. And whenever we make God sad, we must say sorry to Him too, because we know that He is kinder even than that Dentist Mouse, and that He loves us so very much.

CHARITY BEGINS AT HOME

Here is a story about a mouse who did not live in a Church but on a desert island. However, he was almost as poor as a Church Mouse, and so were all his friends and relations. You see they had no bits of cheese to eat, and not even any biscuit crumbs.

One day this mouse was walking along the shore of his island trying to find something for his dinner when he came to a very tall tree; at the top of the tree he saw some big round things, almost like footballs. At once he scrambled up the tree and after a breathless climb he reached one of them and began to gnaw his way into it. It was hard work, but the little mouse was very determined, and kept on muttering sayings to himself like, "If at first you don't succeed, try, try, try again!"

At last he had gnawed a hole which was just big enough for him to squeeze through, and when he got inside, what a sight met his eyes! It was like being in a round room where the walls and ceiling were made of delicious coconut, and the floor of cool, refreshing milk.

"Oh my!" he said to himself, and for a moment he could think of nothing else to say. "Oh my! Oh my! Oh my!" And then he thought to himself, 'There is enough here for all my brothers and sisters and cousins and friends; I had better go to tell them the good news.' But then he thought to himself again and another of those sayings came into his mind, 'Look out for number one; if you don't look after yourself, no one else will.'

For a long time he feasted upon his wonderful discovery, and each time he thought of his friends and relations he quickly thought of a new saying to mutter to himself, such as 'Charity begins at home.' At last he felt that he could really eat no more, but when he tried to squeeze out through the hole that he had made, he found that he had grown too fat, and too lazy to make it any bigger. And so it was, I'm sorry to say, that the poor little mouse never did escape from his coconut prison.

Just as the mouse became imprisoned in the coconut because he was too greedy and too selfish to tell the other mice about it, so boys and girls, and even men and women too, sometimes get imprisoned; not in a coconut, but in the kind of life that they have got used to. 'Being in a rut' I think you call it. Perhaps they have discovered the wonderful news of Jesus and His love for us, but they keep it to themselves instead of telling other people. In time they find that they cannot spread the Good Tidings, even if they want to.

I wonder if that little island mouse would have been alive today if he had remembered another saying to repeat to himself before he had eaten too much of his coconut feast — 'Do as you would be done by'?

RUSSIANS

Oh my fur and whiskers, but wasn't I cross the other day! I knew that there were a lot of apples lying on the ground underneath one of the Rectory trees, and I had been waiting until they were nicely soft and juicy before enjoying them. Then when at last the day came, what do you think I saw? A great flock of birds eating them up!

At first I could scarcely believe my eyes; but when I had blinked hard, and pulled my tail just to make sure that I wasn't dreaming, I looked again, and there they were! Hundreds of them there seemed to be, and each of them trying to eat faster than his neighbour!

"Hi, you!" I spluttered, "what do you think you're doing with my apples?"

It was some time before they heard me, but when they did one of them chirped back, "Why, we didn't know that they were yours; we thought that they belonged to the Rector. In any case there are plenty here; come and help yourself."

Well, of course he was right, and so I ran forward and began to nibble at the first apple that I came to, keeping a wary eye open as I ate, on these strange birds. And strange they were too. They were much too big for sparrows or robins, and much too small for pigeons or rooks. They were the wrong colour for blackbirds or thrushes. And of course they were nothing like my dear old friends the swallows who have flown away from our horrid cold weather to spend their winter in sunny Africa, the lucky things!

"Let me introduce ourselves," said the bird who had spoken before, "we are fieldfares, and you must be a Harvest Mouse?" Oh dearie, dearie me, how ignorant can birds be!

"No," I replied quickly, "I'm not a Harvest Mouse, I'll have you know; I'm a Church Mouse! And so you are fieldfares are you?"

"Yes," he said, "and we've come to stay in this lovely warm country of yours for part of the winter." As he spoke I shuddered, for there had been a sharp frost that night.

'You're welcome!' I thought, as I pictured the swallows basking in the hot tropical sun. But the fieldfare was going on.

"We come from Russia, you know; there the winters are bitterly cold, and the grass is hidden by the snow for months on end. Yes," he twittered as he looked at the lush Rectory grass and weeds, "this is the country for the winter!"

That night, as I lay curled up in my snug little nest and listened to the wind and the rain outside the old Church walls, I longed once again to be with those carefree swallows, or at least for the time when they should come home in the spring. But then I began to think of what the fieldfare had said; after all we have a lot to be thankful for! Before I fell asleep I even found myself thanking God for caring for me as He does, for the feast of apples that I had enjoyed, and for the company in which I ate it.

THE SNOW MOUSE

I am afraid that the poor Field Mice have been having a very hard time of it in this bitter weather, but *we* have been having great fun. You should have seen us having a snowball fight in my Churchyard! It is true that Grandfather didn't join in — he just stood watching us, looking miserable, and muttering, "Whatever next!"

When we got tired of throwing snowballs we decided to make a Snow Mouse. It was hard work and took a long time, but when it was finished we all agreed what a splendid one we had made. He was full size, with an acorn cup for a hat, a match for a stick, and a candle wick for a tail. We built him near to one of the great grey gravestones.

"I wonder if he will last for hundreds of years, like that stone," said Aunt Sarah, "so that one day a mouse of the future may see it and admire our work?"

"We'd better write something in the snow beside him," suggested Freddie of Friesthorpe.

"And we must give him a name," put in Uncle Horace, "what about Horace?"

"Certainly not! whatever next!" snapped Sister Lucy.

And so we busied ourselves writing in the snow — A CHURCH MOUSE. And then, oh my fur and whiskers, but how proud we were! And how we told each other what clever little mice we had been!

Grandfather was not impressed. In fact he was quite nasty about it all. "Vain and silly little mice," he grumbled, "why don't you do something worth while that will really last?"

"What could possibly last longer than this, Grandfather?" asked Phoebe of Faldingworth. "See how strongly we have made him."

"Since you ask," said Grandfather, "suppose you were to invite the Field Mice into your warm nests — that kindness would last a very long time."

"Well," said Bertie, "we will. But this Snow Mouse will last much longer." And that night we did invite the poor, cold Field Mice to share our warmth and our food.

A week later it became much warmer, and we went out into the Churchyard with the Field Mice who were most grateful.

"Thank you for having us," they squeaked.

"It was a pleasure!" we replied, and meant it too.

When we had waved them goodbye we went to admire our Snow Mouse, and Oh! Oh dearie, dearie me! What do you think we found? Just an acorn cup floating forlornly beside a match and a candle wick in a pool of water!

So Grandfather Sebastian had been right as usual!

WAS GOD A BABY?

One cold Christmas Eve a woman and her two children set out from their home to come to the Midnight Service in my dear old Church. Her husband would not come with them because, as he said, "I cannot believe the Christmas story; I cannot believe that God would ever have come into the world as a baby in a stable. Why should He want to do that?"

So his wife and children set off and left him at home by himself. Presently the snow which had been falling steadily, began to come down more and more heavily; the wind rose and howled round the house rattling the doors and window panes and making the fire blaze up right merrily. As he sat there the man thought he heard a tapping at the window, and he hurried over to see what it could be; he pulled aside the curtains and there on the other side of the glass were some bedraggled sparrows, beating against it and trying to get in out of the cruel cold.

The man was a kindly soul and he said to himself, "These poor birds will never be able to live through the night in that blizzard, but what can I do to help them? I know, I'll try to get them to fly into the outhouse." So he quickly put on his overcoat, and scarf, and gloves, and hat, and his great big wellington boots, and with his torch in his hand he stepped outside the warm, comfortable house and tried to shoo the birds into his outhouse. But the more he waved his arms about and shouted at them the more frightened they became. 'They must wonder what on earth I am,' he thought. 'If only I could turn myself into a little bird I could go in and call to them and they would follow me in.'

As he was saying this to himself he heard a familiar sound coming to him faintly over the noise of the storm; it was the Church bells ringing to welcome Christmas Day. Then for the first time in his life he understood how it was that God had chosen to turn Himself into a Baby Boy so that He might lead His people to safety.

I am sure that you understand more of the real meaning of Christmas than I do, because you are oh so very clever, and I am only a poor, rather foolish little Church Mouse. But I think we can all see how it was that God became a Child in Bethlehem, so that men, women and children too, might know Him better, and come to trust and love Him.

CHRISTMAS PARCELS

What a coming and a going there has been amongst us Church Mice this Christmas time, and what an exchanging of presents! I only wish that you could see all the lovely things that I had.

Bertie came to dinner with me on Christmas Day, and brought a matchbox full of crackers, and what fun we had, pulling them and finding out what was inside. Then there were sweets from Lucy, nuts from Aunt Sarah, a very gay tie from Uncle Horace (though I am not sure that I shall dare to wear it, for it is violet with orange spots!) How we admired the wrappings, and enjoyed opening all those parcels!

"You know," said Bertie, as we sat nibbling a piece of cheese which I had borrowed from the Rectory, "these parcels are rather like Church, aren't they?"

"How is that?" I asked, for I couldn't see how they were at all.

"Well," he went on, "you have coloured paper and tinsel or ribbon, and then you take them away and you find your present inside; in the same way you have a Church, and hymns and prayers, and you look to see what they are wrapping up, and you find Jesus — at least you

ought to."

"Well, yes," I said, "I suppose you do."

We sat for a long time dozing pleasantly after our big dinner when we were disturbed by the sound of shuffling feet coming slowly across the Church. "Who can this be?" we wondered. Nearer and nearer came the sound, though very slowly, and then round the corner of a pew we saw — Grandfather Sebastian.

"Why, hallo, Grandfather," we exclaimed, "a merry Christmas to you!"

"Humph!" the old chap muttered. We asked him to sit down and have a bite of something to eat, but he refused, saying that he must be on his way, and out he shuffled.

"Well, I don't know," grumbled Bertie, "how very odd, and not even a present!"

Some time later Bertie himself got up to go, and I went as far as the door with him. When we got there we saw something lying on the floor and ran to find out what it was; it seemed to be a large brown paper bag, which was none too clean, and scrawled across it was written 'With love from Grandfather'.

"Well I never did!" exclaimed Bertie. Hurriedly we opened it, and found that it was filled with the most lovely chocolate, and nuts, and cheese, all mixed up together. "Well I never did!" exclaimed Bertie once again; "there was not much wrapping, but what a lovely present, just the same." As he spoke, we looked back into the Church and saw the Crib. Neither of us spoke, but we both thought the same thing. There may not have been much wrapping — only a poor stable and a mangerful of hay for God's present to us, but what a wonderful present it was!

NO ROOM

I had to do some Christmas shopping, and oh dear me, it was so cold that as I ran along the side of the road my fur became quite stiff with the freezing air. When I got home I thought I saw Grandfather standing there with his white coat and whiskers, until I realized that I was looking in a mirror; it was my own snow-covered reflection that I saw! How we Church Mice hate the cold winters, and how we snuggle up in our little nests to try to keep warm! How sorry we are for ourselves, and how badly treated we think we are!

Now on that evening, just before Christmas, when the frost lay thick upon the ground, and the trees were glistening white through the driving snow, I was curled up in my soft, warm little nest with some biscuit crumbs beside me, just in case I felt hungry. I was cosy and comfortable, and meant to stay where I was all night, and perhaps some of the next day too.

But just as I was dropping off to sleep I heard a scuffling and a scratching at the door of my Church.

"Oh dearie, dearie me!" I exclaimed, "whoever can that be?" and rather crossly I scrambled out of my nest and went to let in whoever it was. "Could it be Aunt Sarah with her children?" I wondered. "Or perhaps Sister Lucy?" But when I opened the door they were not Church Mice at all who came stumbling in, stamping their feet, and blowing on their paws. They were a family of Field Mice! Oh my paws and tail, but wasn't I angry! What right had they to come here? It was my Church not theirs! They never gave me any of their corn at harvest time, so why should I give them shelter now? As like as not they were unbaptized too!

I was just going to say, "I'm sorry, there's no room here," when I saw out of the corner of my eye the Christmas Crib. And then I remembered how once, long ago, there had been no room in the inn for Mary and Joseph, and how the Baby Jesus had been born in a stable. "No room?" I asked myself. "Of course there is room, plenty of it." So I hastened to make them welcome, took them into my snug little home under the pulpit, and set before them a really good and satisfying meal.

Then a strange thing happened. I saw through a crack in the floor that the Church which had been cold and forbidding had become warm and friendly. The light from the Crib seemed to burn more brightly, and I felt more at home, more content than I could ever remember feeling before. The little strangers who had come in from their cruelly cold fields were strangers no more, but friends who by their very presence were adding to the warmth around me. Not Church Mice certainly, but still children of the same Father in Heaven who loves us all.

I wonder if you are like me, and know of people who need your love and friendship, as those poor Field Mice needed mine? If so, then never say that you have no room in your heart for them, else how can you have a place for the Babe of Bethlehem?

OF GREAT PRICE

Last year we all went to a party at Uncle Horace's Church in Holton, and oh my, but didn't we have a lovely time! Hide-and-seek under the pews! Pass the Parcel in the pulpit, and Blind Mouse's Buff in the belfry! Then what a wonderful feast Uncle Horace had for us! And afterwards what an opening of presents! Everyone gave everyone else a present, and I haven't got room to describe the chocolates, and the nuts, and the biscuits, and all the cheeses! But I must tell you what Grandfather Sebastian gave to young Mickie and Minnie.

Each had a parcel done up in the prettiest paper, and Mickie opened his first; inside was the most delicious looking box of chocolates, and how our mouths did water as we looked at them! Mickie was so delighted that he almost forgot to say, "Thank you very much, Grandfather."

Then it was Minnie's turn. Her parcel was quite a big one, and we all watched as she tore off the ribbon and the coloured paper. Inside there was a layer of soft tissue which she quickly pulled away, but still there was more, layers and layers of it. At last she came to the middle, and

there lying in its nest of the softest down was a little, round, white thing.

"What is it?" asked Minnie, and then she squeaked with surprise as she tried to bite it, for it was as hard as stone.

"You'll have to find out for yourself what it is," Grandfather told her; and we could see that the old mouse was unhappy that she was not really pleased with her present, even though she said "Thank you" most politely.

Soon it was Christmas Day, and we heard again the story of how a Baby was born in a stable. His Mother knew who He was, and so did some shepherds and wise men. But many people didn't understand what a wonderful gift God had given us when He sent His Son into the world to show how He loves us. When the Baby grew up they were unkind to Him because they still didn't know who He was.

It was some weeks later that Grandfather had a visit from a very old friend of his who lived in a very old shop near the Cathedral; in his shop he sold jewellery and precious stones.

"Tell me," said this old mouse, "what did you do with that precious pearl you bought long ago?" I don't know if Grandfather heard him, for he said nothing. He just sat there with a rather wistful expression on his old face. Perhaps he was wondering when Minnie would learn the true value of the present which he had given her.

THE FOURTH WISE MOUSE

Once upon a time there were three wise mice. They lived some miles away from here in very grand holes where everything was of the best. Their nests were soft and warm, their coats were sleek and spotless, and their tummies were always well filled with satisfying food. They were good and kind, and were respected by their friends and neighbours.

These wise mice were able to look up at the stars, and to understand from them what God was telling them; so it was that one night when they saw a new star they agreed to follow it. All through the night they travelled across fields, over bridges, along country roads until at last they came in the early morning to an old village Church. Through the stained glass windows the light shone out in lovely colours, and through the open door they saw a Christmas Crib. So it was that those three wise mice scrambled up into the sweet smelling hay of the Crib, and laid their gifts down in front of the tiny Baby, a figure no bigger than they were; gifts of corn, and bread, and chocolate.

Meanwhile, some distance away lived another mouse, as wise as the first three. He too lived comfortably, his nest was snug, his clothes fine, and his food ample. He saw the same star, and also set off with his gifts. He had three pieces of cheese to bring, for which he had had to pay very dearly, from the old shop mouse down his lane.

He had not gone far however, before he saw a fierce rat shouting at some little mice to give him all their store of food; for a moment the fourth wise mouse hesitated, for he did so wish to bring his three pieces of cheese as a gift; but then he made up his mind and called out to the rat, "Here, take this, and leave these poor mice alone," and sadly went on his way.

For a time he walked on, wondering what he would find at the end of his journey, when he heard a faint crying from the hedgerow. He peered in, and there he saw a family of young mice crying for their mother whom they had not seen for days.

"Why," he called out to them, "we can't have this! Here's a lump of cheese for you." He enjoyed helping them, but then he remembered that he only had one piece left to take with him on his journey.

For an hour he trudged on until he saw in the distance softly coloured light streaming from the windows of the old village Church, and he hurried on with his one remaining gift. So eager was he to get there, that he never saw the thin old Field Mouse until he bumped into him.

"I'm sorry friend," he said at once, but the old mouse was too weak to reply and just looked up at him with his great sad eyes from the ground where he lay. With a heavy heart our traveller gave his last piece of cheese to this starving stranger.

Slowly he went on, up the Church path, in through the old oak door, and into the Church where stood the Crib. He saw the figures of Mary and Joseph there, with between them the Baby Christ Child, and beside the manger lay some little bits of corn, and bread, and chocolate. For a moment the fourth wise mouse stood there with tears in his eyes, knowing that he had come empty-handed; but then quite suddenly as he waited in the hay, beside the little figures of the Christmas Crib, he seemed to hear a voice.

"Well done, my little mouse; the gifts you gave, you gave to me, you know."

Although he was wise, he was only a very little mouse, and he had been afraid. But now his fear was gone, and he knew that giving to those in need, whether they be lonely and frightened little creatures of the wild, or children starving in some foreign land, will bring joy to the God who was once a Child in Bethlehem.

AMERICA AND BACK

The Gypsy Mouse and I were sitting in the dark one night when the Church door opened, and a young boy came in. Through the dark he came, feeling his way, but soon he was quite lost, and when the Gypsy Mouse called out, "Hallo," he jumped back against a pew, and it was some time before he found the door again and went out.

"Well," said I, "it's funny how people cannot see in the dark, nor find their way without maps and compasses; they could learn a thing or two from my old friends the swallows."

"That reminds me," replied the Gypsy Mouse, "of a true tale told me by a sea-bird called a Manx shearwater."

"One night," the shearwater had said, "I was sitting by my nest on the Welsh island of Skokholm. My wife was sitting on the nest with our young chick and all seemed quiet and peaceful, when suddenly, a large net was thrown over me and I was a prisoner. I flapped my wings wildly, but the more I struggled the more I became entangled in the net.

"Presently I heard a kindly voice saying, 'There, there, my beauty, keep still and you'll not get hurt.' The man quickly had me clear of the net and in a box with a bed of soft grass inside it. I was still very frightened but sat down and waited to see what would happen next. Well, the man scrambled down the cliff with me, carried me over the beach to a small boat, and we were on our way across the sea. When we landed I was put in a car and driven off into the night and at last into an airport; very frightened I was by all the noise and by the bright lights; lots of people stared at me, and I stared back at them.

"The next thing that I remember was being put into an aeroplane, and for hour after hour we flew across the sea until we landed in America, in the State of Massachusetts. A tiny ring had been put round one of my legs, but I had been well treated with plenty of fish to eat. At last they took the lid off the box, and a funny voice said, 'Waal little bird, off you go!'

"I needed no second telling. After a quick look round I was off, and in my mind was just one thought, to get home as fast as ever I could. Something inside me told me which way to go and I never hesitated. After a time I saw the great greeny waters of the Atlantic Ocean spreading out before me, and I knew that home lay ahead. For days and nights I flew on; sometimes the sea was calm, sometimes so rough that I sheared the water with my wings, while the wind did its best to drive me off my course. But at last I saw the familiar rocks of Skokholm and I knew that I was home. What a welcome I had from my wife and chick. Presently I looked around and saw two men sitting on a nearby rock watching us through field-glasses.

" 'Remarkable,' I heard one of them say, 'just twelve days since he set off from America!' "

Well that is the true story that the Gypsy Mouse from Wales told me, as he had heard it from that brave little Manx shearwater. What a wonderful instinct God has given to so many of his creatures!

AM I A PUPPET?

I wonder what the longest word is that you have ever heard? I used to think that Gorgonzola was the longest, and certainly the best one. Gorgonzola cheese sounds so nice, it tastes so delicious, and it smells — well we mice like the smell anyway!

But then I heard another word the other day that was much longer than Gorgonzola. It was Predestination, and I wonder if you know what that means. I certainly didn't, so when the Rector came into the Church I squeaked out, "Hey!" and he gave a great big jump!

"I do wish you wouldn't do that," he said rather sharply.

"Sorry," I said, "but I want to know what a very long word means."

"And what very long word is that?" he asked, so I told him.

"Predestination," I said.

"Goodness me, wherever did you hear that?" he said.

"Never mind where I heard it," I retorted rather rudely, "just tell me what it means; that is if you can."

Well, he sat down and he talked for ages, and I'm afraid that I cannot remember very much of what he said, but I think that what he was

trying to say was this. A destination is where you are going to on a journey; if you get on a bus in Wickenby your destination may be Market Rasen. Predestination means that your journey is planned ahead, so that you would have to go to Market Rasen whether you wanted to or not; you would not be allowed to get off for a bit of cheese with Sister Lucy as the bus went through Lissington.

"People who believe in Predestination," he went on, "believe that our life in this world is like a journey which has been planned by God, that God knows what is going to happen, and nothing that we do can alter it."

This sounded rather a good idea to me. I had always believed it was wrong to run over to the Rectory and help myself to a snack from the larder; but if God has planned everything that I do, then surely He could not object — even if the Rector might!

"I know what you are thinking," laughed the Rector, "it is a difficult thing to understand, but I think that God could rule the world with a rod of iron, if He wished, and force everyone to do His will; in that case He would stop you running over to my larder for that piece of cheese which I am saving for my own supper!" He stopped for a moment, and then continued, "I believe that He could force us to be good, but in fact He prefers to let us rule our own lives, and He just hopes that we shall choose the right ways and not the wrong ways."

That evening I ran across to the Rectory larder — just to *look* you understand — when I heard a song being sung on the wireless. It had a lovely tune, and it was all about a puppet on a string, who had to do just what he was told. 'No,' I thought to myself, 'I am not a puppet on a string. I can choose myself whether I am going to be a good mouse, or a bad one, although of course, I shall have to ask God to help me.'

THE ELECTION

One day last week a funny little mouse came to my Church. I had never seen him before, but he seemed to know my name. "Ah, William my good friend, delighted to see you!" he said, as he shook me vigorously by the paw. He was dressed much as other mice are, except that he wore a large rosette made up of all the colours of the rainbow, and as big as a penny piece. "Let me introduce myself," he said, "I am a Parliamentary Mouse, and I belong to the 'Free Cheese' Party. I have come to ask if I may count on your vote in the election." Much of what he said was too hard for me to understand, but one thing did make me sit up and take notice. "If you vote for me I will promise that all Church Mice will have as much cheese as they can manage to eat!"

Soon after he had gone my various relations began appearing at the door, all very excited, and all talking at once. It seemed that other Parliamentary Mice had called upon them, and each one had worn a different coloured rosette. In fact Uncle Horace was so taken with the pale lilac one which his visitor was wearing that he promised to vote for him on the spot. And it wasn't only their rosettes that were different, so were their promises. Mine as you know promised free cheese, another promised a ban on poison and traps; yet another said that he would make a law that all cats should wear bells, so that we would hear them coming.

How happy we all were, and how we laughed and chattered about the good days to come, and how eager we were to vote for these kind Parliamentary Mice and their promises! But then in the very middle of our merriment, there was a soft noise by the door of the Church, and in shuffled Grandfather Sebastian. He looked older than ever, and very solemn, and there was absolutely no sign of merriment on his face. When we had explained to him why we were so happy a rather wry smile came to his lips.

"No more traps or poison?" he said. "As much cheese as you want?" he said. "Cats with bells on?" he said. And I think he would have added "Ring the other one!" had he known the expression! We sat round in a circle feeling a little bit ashamed of ourselves.

"Now you just listen to me," he went on, "if you want to avoid being caught in a trap, you must be alert and keep your eyes open. If you want to avoid poisoned food, you must not be greedy. And as for cats with bells — well!" After a bit he went on, "By all means vote for a

Parliamentary Mouse, but remember that it is by your own efforts and not by listening to promises that life will become better." He was speaking more quietly now, and we had to strain our ears to hear what it was that he was saying.

"I don't believe that any of you mentioned God or how to serve Him better, in all this talk. Does He not count for anything in your plans? And nor did I hear any mention of the poor Field Mice. I hope that you are not all thinking only of yourselves."

TRUTH

One of the things that Pontius Pilate said to Jesus was, "What is truth?" Perhaps you think that a funny sort of question to ask, but it is not an easy one to answer — what is truth?

Young Mickie was making an awful noise in Snelland Church and when Aunt Sarah said, "Who is making that noise?" he replied "Minnie." Now that was not the truth. Then Sister Lucy was feeling very wretched; she had a bad cold and headache, but when she was asked, "How are you?" she replied, "Oh, not too bad thank you." And that was not the truth either, but somehow it did not seem quite so bad as Mickie's answer.

We were all discussing such things over a bite of supper in my Church one evening. "I once heard of a little boy," said Uncle Horace, "who made his mother very cross because he would keep on saying that he had seen a lion in the next door garden, when really and truly they both knew that it was an Alsatian dog. At last his mother got tired of this and said 'Go to your room, and tell God that you are sorry for saying such things.' So the boy went to his room and after a while came back.

'Well,' said his mother, 'and did you say sorry to God?' 'Yes,' said the boy, 'and God said to me, "Do you know, I've often mistaken that dog for a lion myself!" ' "

"What is truth, Grandfather?" we asked, turning as usual to the only one of us who was wise enough to give an answer. But Grandfather Sebastian sat there saying nothing.

At last he replied, "Jesus gave no answer to that question."

"But Grandfather," persisted Freddie of Friesthorpe, "is it always right to tell the truth, even if it hurts someone else, or seems unkind?"

"The truth is always right," said Grandfather, "but it is not just the opposite of a lie. It is as wrong to hurt someone unnecessarily as it is to tell a lie." This seemed strange coming from Grandfather, for we all knew that he is inclined to be a bad tempered old mouse with a very sharp tongue!

"What do you mean, Grandfather?" asked Uncle Horace.

"What do I mean?" he retorted. "I should have thought that even as stupid a mouse as you are, would understand!"

Then, with a smile on his wrinkled old cheeks, he went on more gently, "Being true means telling the truth of course, but it means a lot more as well. It means being honourable and just and fair. I don't know about people, or what a dictionary would say," he went on, "but for a Church Mouse the truth must have just a taste of kindness." At this his eyes twinkled as he turned to me. "And talking of taste, young William, where's that rare old Gorgonzola cheese which you promised us?"

FREE CHEESE IN A MOUSETRAP

Once upon a time there was a Very Moral Mouse who was given to repeating moral sayings to anyone who would listen to him. "Look before you leap," he used to say; and, "He who hesitates is lost." "Many hands make light work," and, "Too many cooks spoil the broth." But the saying that I remember best was this, "There is always free cheese in a mousetrap!"

Well now, I know how very clever and intelligent you are, dear reader! And I know how much more clever you are than poor Uncle Horace used to be when he was a young mouse. For you would understand what that Very Moral Mouse had meant when he said, "There is always free cheese in a mousetrap!" But do you think Uncle Horace understood? Not he!

It was on a Wednesday at the beginning of Lent, Ash Wednesday I think you call it, that the Very Moral Mouse had climbed up into the pulpit, just like the Rector does; and on to the pulpit ledge, which is not what the Rector does! And like the Rector, he had tried to look very good and very holy. He held his paws just so, and said in a loud voice,

"This is my text; 'There is always free cheese in a mousetrap!' "

Now had Uncle Horace not eaten a very large dinner that Ash Wednesday, and had he not washed it down with a whole thimbleful of elderberry wine, all might have been well; he would have heard lots of long words like temptation and confession and forgiveness, and even some short ones like sin and sorrow and love. But poor Uncle Horace heard none of this for he was fast asleep!

When he woke up all that he could remember was the last thing that he had heard, "There is always free cheese in a mousetrap!" He was peckish after his sleep and said to himself, "Free cheese! Aha, that's just what I want. And what's more, I know where there is a mousetrap!"

Sure enough, there beside the Altar was a trap in which was the most tempting piece of cheese, and on it there was a little price tag which said 'FREE'. Oh, my fur and whiskers, but wasn't he delighted! And didn't he lick his lips! And didn't he snatch for that tempting piece of cheese!

Well . . . you know the rest of the story, how poor, silly greedy Uncle Horace was caught by the tail! All the rest of us only just managed to pull him away, and oh my, but wasn't his tail sore! Grandfather Sebastian was not at all amused.

"You're a very foolish young mouse to give in to temptation like that," he said. "And there are many other things in a mouse's life which may be free, but are certainly bad for him," he said, "like cheese in traps, or cats."

A KESTREL

Here is a true tale and the Rector will vouch for its truth if you care to ask him. It happened like this.

Grandfather Sebastian was having a quiet stroll around his Churchyard in Snarford, thinking how peaceful it was, and not looking forward to the noise and bustle of the Harvest Festival, when suddenly he had a strange feeling — not so much in his head as in his tummy; you know the kind of feeling that your tummy gets when you leave it behind on that humpback bridge at Langworth. And his tummy went like that because he felt he was being watched!

At once he stopped in his tracks and froze to the ground. Then very cautiously he looked in front of him, then to his left, then to his right, then behind him, but nothing could he see. Then, very, very slowly he looked up, and there — high above the top of the Church tower, he saw it, and it was a dark shape hovering in the air.

As he saw it, so it saw him, and down it swooped; down, down it came right to where he had been standing only a split whisker of time before. But Grandfather was no fool; he had darted into the long grass, and now was running as fast as his poor old legs would carry him, to the Church door. Someone had left it open, and he tottered in quite out of breath, followed by a rush of wings!

Most of you will know what a kestrel is like — with long pointed wings, cruel claws, a horrid hooked bill, and an appetite for mice! Picture then, poor old Grandfather's plight, as he cowered under a pew while the kestrel searched for him!

Then mercifully some Americans came in to see the tombs. Grandfather has never liked these tombs because they encourage visitors to come to see them, and to disturb his peace; but this time he was glad enough, for the kestrel promptly forgot all about him, and flew up onto a rafter, while he was able to scramble down his hole to safety, hearing as he went a voice saying, "Gee, a genuyne English Church Mouse!"

That is not quite the end of the story, for when those Americans left the Church, they closed the door behind them, and there was the kestrel shut in Grandfather's own Church, and there he remained until two days later when the Rector happened to come in and find him there. By then that kestrel was weak with thirst, and the Rector had no difficulty in shooing him out of the door into the open air, where he soon recovered.

"Why," said I when Grandfather told me all this, "why didn't the Rector kill that awful bird?"

"For two reasons," he replied. "First, because a kestrel is as much one of God's creatures as you or I, and is loved by God, even though he may not be a very holy or Churchy bird."

"You said there were two reasons," I prompted.

"Well," said the old mouse with a twinkle in his eye, "between you and me, young William my mouse, I rather think that the Rector too was just a teeny weeny bit afraid of those cruel claws and that hooked bill!"

THE FAMILY PHOTOGRAPH

Not long ago we decided to have a family photograph taken. Grandfather Sebastian was disgusted, but finally agreed to come along with the rest of us to the Camera Mouse. Mickie and Minnie were very excited. Young Phoebe of Faldingworth is still a bit coquettish although she is now married, and was highly delighted. But of course it was Uncle Horace of Holton, resplendent in an orange waistcoat and green bow-tie who was the best pleased — though as you boys and girls would say, "The gilt was taken from the gingerbread," when he was told that the picture would be in black and white!

The Camera Mouse lived in an old barn behind some sacks. The studio, as he called it, was a large room, at least three feet long, and in it were a number of screens and lots of lights. In the middle of the room was a strange object covered with a black cloth. The Camera Mouse was a dapper little fellow with very black whiskers, and a white coat.

It took a long time to get us all properly arranged; just when he thought we looked right, Mickie and Minnie would begin to pinch each other, or Uncle Horace would take out a pocket mirror to admire himself. Once, when everything really did seem set, Grandfather took a pinch of snuff which started him off sneezing and the rest of us shaking with laughter! Sister Lucy, meanwhile, looked more disapproving with every moment that passed.

At last however, all was ready and the Camera Mouse dived under the cloth, where we assumed the camera was hidden. Presently he popped out again looking very fierce, and squeaked, "Be natural!" We had all been sitting quietly, and to be natural we had to twitch our noses, scratch our ears, and waggle our tails. Just as we were feeling really natural a further sharp little squeak came from under the black cloth, "Be still!"

Have you ever tried to be still while you are twitching your noses, scratching your ears, and waggling your tails? . . . . no, I don't suppose you have! Well, we did the best we could to twitch and scratch and waggle, and at the same time to be still, but it wasn't easy! Then once more there came a sharp command, "Smile!"

"Stuff and nonsense!" exploded Grandfather, who had been getting crosser and crosser, "what a waste of time!" It took several minutes to pacify him, but at last the photo was taken and we hurried outside.

As we walked along the farm lane, Grandfather began to mumble softly to himself. "Odd," he was saying, "those words that that stupid young mouse was saying; they remind me of a sermon I heard many years ago in the Cathedral; it was about prayer."

"Be natural," the preacher had said. "Don't be too stiff and formal and unfriendly when you pray. Be still; seek some quiet place and time, and turn in that quiet and peace to God. Smile; don't frown at God; He is happy to hear you, be happy when you speak to Him. Be natural. Be still. Smile!"

"I don't know, I'm sure," went on Grandfather Sebastian. "That's true for prayer, but you won't catch me going to have my photo taken again all the same! Impudent young whippersnapper . . . " and the grumbling didn't stop until the old mouse was safe home in Snarford, nor did the grousing!

HENRIETTA HEDGEHOG

If the Queen were to send you a postcard saying 'What about dropping in for a cup of tea?' you would treat her invitation as a royal command, and go! When Grandfather Sebastian looked into my Church last week and said, "What about a walk?" I went! Mind you, it was a lovely evening; the blackbirds and thrushes were seeing which could give the best song; the larks were singing fit to burst, and a cuckoo went on and on, cuckooing and cuckooing.

As we walked slowly along the side of the road a family of Field Mice called out, "Good-evening Grandfather Sebastian," very politely, and a large hare gave us a friendly grin as he scampered away.

And then . . . there was very nearly a horrible accident. At the same time as we heard the distant roar of a motor car, we saw a funny little bundle of spikes come waddling over the road towards us calling out, "Hallo there, wait for me, it's Henrietta Hedgehog." As she made her way over the road, oh so slowly, the distant roar of the motor car grew louder and nearer, oh so quickly! Grandfather and I dodged into the long grass well off the road, and out of the way of the great monster

which was rushing along towards us. But as we reached safety Henrietta reached the middle of the road, and did the most extraordinary thing; she rolled herself into a ball, stuck out all her prickles and sat down! Nearer and nearer came the motor car, and more and more bristly did Henrietta look as she sat there in its path. Then . . . whoosh . . . it had gone, missing her by a whisker's width. Slowly she unrolled herself and continued her dignified journey across the road.

"There," she exclaimed, "it was afraid to touch me, you see!"

We tried to explain that the car was certainly not afraid of her, and that she would surely get run over if she behaved like that again; but I don't believe she paid any attention to what we were saying.

When we got home to my Church, and after Grandfather had enjoyed a piece of Stilton cheese, he sat back and told me about Henrietta and her family.

"They are very stupid, you know," he said. "For hundreds of years they have protected themselves from their enemies by rolling up into prickly balls, and now they think that doing so will save them from being run over by a motor car!"

Late that night I lay awake in my nest, thinking of silly Henrietta Hedgehog, and how young hedgehogs must be ready to face new dangers which their parents and grandparents knew nothing about. I suppose the same thing is true for boys and girls, and even Church Mice. We must all be ready to face new dangers and new temptations when they come. Often this will mean using new and modern ways and ideas, but always there will be the same God caring for us, and helping us in our lives.

COCK CROW

It was a regular family evening, and after supper we gathered round while Grandfather Sebastian talked to us. He went on for a very long time in his rather monotonous old voice and Aunt Sarah almost fell asleep listening; Freddie sat there with his eyes tight shut, but promised that he was awake.

Grandfather was reminding us how St. Peter had told Jesus that he would never desert Him, or run away; Jesus had replied, "You will be so frightened that three times you will say you don't know me, before the cock has time to crow in the morning!" Grandfather went on to say how offended Peter was, and declared that he would never, never deny Jesus.

"And did he?" asked Freddie who was awake by this time.

"Did he indeed!" interrupted Lucy. "Of course he did."

"Yes," muttered old Grandfather, "I'm afraid he did. A maidservant teased him, and her friends laughed at him, 'You're a friend of Jesus!' they jeered. Three times Peter declared 'I don't even know Him,' and then . . . the cock crew. As it did so Jesus passed by and looked at him, and Peter was so ashamed that he burst into tears."

At last the story had come to an end.

"Well," said Uncle Horace, "I may not be a very good Church Mouse, but at least I would never deny being one; I wouldn't say that I don't know Jesus." Grandfather looked at him quietly for a moment from beneath his shaggy old eyebrows.

"No?" he whispered softly. And then, after a long pause went on, as though to himself, "I wonder."

By now it was early morning, and we were feeling rather peckish. "What about going to look for something to eat?" I suggested, and they all agreed except Grandfather who said that it was time he was getting home. As we made our way into the Churchyard all was quiet and still; the night was dark except for the first grey signs of dawn over the Wolds.

"Follow me," I said softly, and led them over the road and into the Rectory hen house. There were the hens roosting over our heads and there before us was a welcome trough of mash. By now Uncle Horace who loves his food almost as much as his clothes, was ahead of us and quickly jumped right into the trough. And then . . . oh, my fur and whiskers! What a noise there was! He had landed right on top of three big Farm Mice who were there before us!

"How dare you!" they squeaked at him. "Go back to your Church and leave this to us."

"But," replied Uncle Horace in a shaky voice, while we stayed out of sight listening very hard, "but I'm a Farm Mouse like you — I'm no Church Mouse."

"Of course you're a Church Mouse," they repeated, but again he denied that he was.

Then one of them said, "You're a Church Mouse, and you believe in Jesus don't you?"

"Of course I don't," laughed Uncle Horace, "believe in Jesus, me? What an idea!"

No sooner had he spoken than the old cockerel gave out an ear-piercing shriek just above our heads, "Cock-a-doodle-doo!" he cried. As the sounds died away we saw the bowed old figure of Grandfather Sebastian stumbling up the road on his long walk home. Uncle Horace never said another word; he crept past us and went slowly out into the early morning light. Never had his lilac coloured waistcoat or his foppish ways seemed more pathetic, and it was a long time before we saw him again.

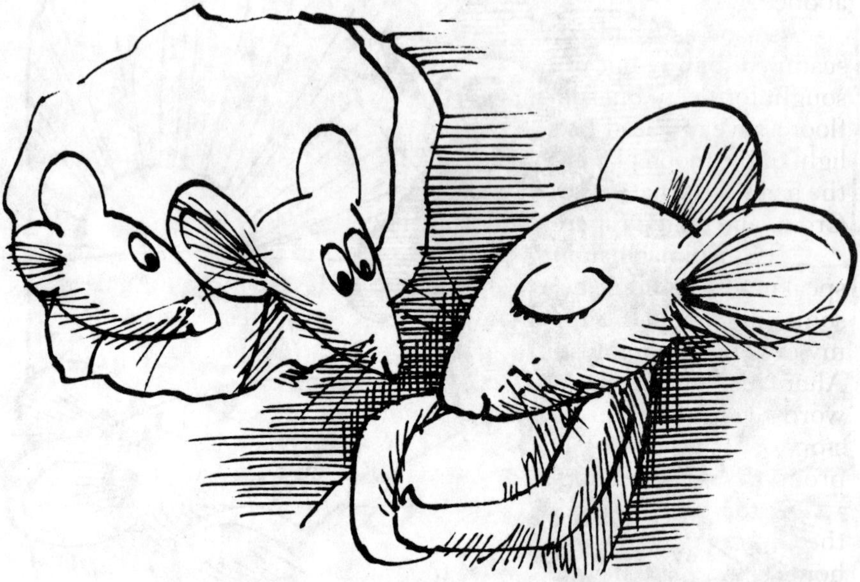

A HELPING PAW

One evening, after I had had my supper, a thin little face that was none too clean peeped down into my hole, and a little voice squeaked, "Oh please Mister Church Mouse, we are sorry to disturb you, but please will you come and help us?" And as he was speaking another thin and rather grubby little face appeared beside him.

Well! I was not at all pleased — would you have been? After a hard day's work eating all the scraps of cheese that I could lay my paws on, I had just settled down for a comfortable snooze when I was interrupted like this!

"No!" I said sternly, "I am much too busy," and I closed my eyes tight shut, so that I could not see the unwelcome visitors.

"But please, Mister Church Mouse," they insisted, "our home got damaged in the storm, and we don't seem to be able to mend it ourselves. Please help us to make it tidy and clean again."

"Whatever next!" I exclaimed, opening my eyes and sitting up. "What impudence you have, asking a respectable Church Mouse to clean up the nasty, dirty home of some Field Mice! Be off with you at once!"

As soon as I had sat up the two Field Mice took to their heels and scampered away out of my Church. I very soon lay down again, and sought for sleep, but somehow I couldn't find it. Through a crack in the floor above my head I could see a sparkle of gold; it must have been the light of the moon playing on the Altar Cross. I closed my eyes to shut out the sight, but that was even worse; now I seemed to see a great wooden Cross, and on it a Figure, looking at me, oh so sadly!

"It's just imagination!" I said to myself, but then I heard the Figure speaking; I couldn't hear every word for He spoke softly, but it was something about a Supper and washing people's feet. When I opened my eyes the moon must have gone in for there was no sparkle from the Altar, just a great black darkness. As I lay there I wondered what the words could have meant, and slowly an old story came back to me, a story of Jesus washing His Disciples' feet, and telling us never to be too proud to serve one another.

By this time I was wide awake. I scrambled out of my nest, ran out to the Churchyard and over to the paddock where the Field Mice had their home. How glad they were to see me, and oh, my fur and whiskers, but what fun we had mending their poor old nest! They tried to thank me, but I knew that I did not deserve this and hurried home, happy, and ready for bed.

Do you think it was just a dream that made me believe I saw that Figure again? And do you think I really heard Him whisper, "Well done, my little Church Mouse"?

DOUBTS

Recently Thomas of Torrington looked in to admire our Easter Garden. As it happened, Sarah and her children had come over from Snelland to share my dinner when he appeared, so we asked him to join us.

We talked about the usual things that Church Mice do talk about, such as cheese, and bread, and chocolate, and more cheese.

"Did you get any Easter Eggs this year?" I asked Mickie.

"Oh yes," he replied, "they had sugary Smarties inside!"

"Fancy talking like that!" exclaimed Thomas. "Sarah you shouldn't let them talk such nonsense!"

"Nonsense?" she enquired, puzzled.

"Well," went on Thomas, "whoever heard of an egg with sugary Smarties inside!"

I knew that Thomas was very poor, but I could hardly believe that he had never seen an Easter Egg. "Thomas," I said, "surely you used to have Easter Eggs when you were younger?"

"Of course I did," he replied rather crossly, "but they were no different from other eggs except that the hens laid them on Easter Day.

Eggs with Smarties inside them indeed! Whoever heard of anything so ridiculous!"

Sarah and I looked at each other, and Mickie nudged Minnie so that she began to giggle. "There are such things, you know," Sarah persisted, "and very nice they are too!"

But Thomas would not believe us. "Rubbish," he snorted, "complete rubbish!" And then he went on, "Unless I can actually see one, I will not believe it."

Mickie and Minnie had long since finished their eggs, but it seemed possible that there might be one left over at the farm. So it was that we all went to find out. On the way we passed the Rectory hens, and it seemed to me that Thomas was eyeing them very suspiciously, as though he half expected to see a chocolate egg come rolling out of the hen house. It was broad daylight so we had to beware of the farm cats, but in the end we found what we were looking for — an egg wrapped in silver paper. It was only a matter of minutes before we discovered that it was indeed made of chocolate, and full of sugary Smarties.

"Well now," gasped Thomas, "whoever would have thought it!"

That evening when they had all gone home, Grandfather looked in for a few moments and I told him of Thomas and his doubts. "It's strange," the old mouse muttered, "that his name should have been Thomas."

"Strange?" I asked. "Why?"

"Well," went on Grandfather, "surely you know how Jesus, who died upon the Cross rose to life again on the first Easter Sunday?"

"Yes," I said, "but what has that got to do . . . ?"

"Don't interrupt," grumbled Grandfather, "now where was I? Oh yes . . . . The disciples were gathered together when Jesus came to them after He had risen from the dead and only Thomas was away. When the disciples told him that they had seen Jesus, he said that was absurd, and that he would not believe unless he could see for himself. A week later Jesus appeared again, and this time Thomas was there as well, and was delighted when he saw Jesus; but Jesus said to him, 'Thomas because thou hast seen me, thou hast believed; blessed are they that have not seen, and yet have believed!'

"You see," went on Grandfather, "poor old doubting Thomas would not believe that Jesus had risen from the dead until he had seen Him with his own eyes. You and I cannot see Jesus, but we can still believe that He rose to life again, and it's good to remember those words 'Blessed are they that have not seen, and yet have believed'."

ALIVE FOR EVERMORE

It was Easter, and we were invited to a party in Snarford Church. We were all there. Myself of course, William of Wickenby. Freddie of Friesthorpe holding paws with Phoebe of Faldingworth. Sister Lucy of Lissington as prim and disapproving as ever. Uncle Horace of Holton in a brand new primrose coloured suit with a magenta waistcoat! Aunt Sarah of Snelland with Mickie and Minnie, full of mischief. Sir Bertram de Buslingthorpe, known to his friends as Bertie with a match sized shooting stick. And of course Grandfather Sebastian.

Grandfather welcomed us all in his gruff rather fierce way. He glowered at Uncle Horace's suit but didn't say anything. The old mouse must have been very busy, for he had provided a wonderful spread on the monument behind the Altar; I fear there were soon crumbs of Gorgonzola cheese all over the knight's face.

Afterwards, while we sat and talked, and Mickie and Minnie played hide-and-seek, and Uncle Horace kept on eating chocolate cake, we thought of all the adventures we had had. Of Jezebel the Rectory cat, of the kestrel that had got caught in that very Church. Of Field Mice in the snow and of my old friends the swallows who should be soon home again.

Grandfather was very quiet, and when Aunt Sarah asked if he was all right, he didn't answer, but just sat there with a rather unusually gentle expression on his lined old face. She gave him a soft nudge, and he toppled over, resting on the armour of the knight. Sister Lucy tried to rouse him, and then our hearts became as cold as that of the old stone knight as we realized that Grandfather Sebastian was dead. That wonderfully frightening, dear, kind, bad-tempered old mouse was no more!

Oh dearie, dearie me! But what a funeral we had; and how we cried; and how we all said how gentle, and good, and kind he had always been. And then . . . when we thought it was all over, we got the fright of our lives! Oh, my fur and whiskers but didn't we just! For there came a voice, it seemed from nowhere. It was as grumpy and grousy as ever, as it said in the old familiar tone, "Stuff and nonsense!" And we knew that Grandfather Sebastian like His Saviour whom he had always loved in that funny way of his, was alive, and will live for evermore.

SEBASTIAN
MOUSE